Neal Brown

Critical Confessions

Neal Brown
Critical Confessions
ISBN/EAN: 9783743340442
Manufactured in Europe, USA, Canada, Australia, Japa
Cover: Foto ©Lupo / pixelio.de

Manufactured and distributed by brebook publishing software (www.brebook.com)

Neal Brown

Critical Confessions

CRITICAL CONFESSIONS

By NEAL BROWN

THE PHILOSOPHER PRESS
WAUSAU WISCONSIN

CONTENTS

	PAGE
ANDREW LANG,	1
HONORE DE BALZAC,	18
WILLIAM MAKEPEACE THACKERAY,	27
DEGENERATION,	69
JOHN SMITH,	116
A DEFERRED CRITICISM,	171
AMERICAN NOTES,	201
AMERICANISM IN LITERATURE,	223

CRITICAL CONFESSIONS

ANDREW LANG

In pessimistic mood, one feels that the world of letters has squandered most of its genius, and is traveling toward an intellectual poorhouse. The great poets have certainly departed. Stevenson has gone, and there are but two or three story-tellers left. Fiction has become short and choppy; a matter of fragments, without sustained flights. The few mountain peaks that are left are nodding. The fruits of letters seem over-ripe and ready to fall rotting to the ground. It is a transition time, and perhaps the soil is being fertilized by the rank growths that spring up, for something better to come.

We are seduced from healthy standards by *fin de siecle* tendencies; the color of nature is gone, and we have green carnations and unsubstantial, unreal things. Men are made to seem like shadows walking. We are non-creative. We either imitate, or else we rebel against imitation, and the pendulum swings as far the other way. The result is strange, uncouth, fancies in art and literature, and our romancists make monkeys of men, to borrow a phrase from the vernacular. The commercial autocrats of magazinedom, and certain of the hack writers of newspaperdom set the fashion. With the small arts of puffery they build up small reputations that die in a day. How often the announcement; "a genius is coming, watch for him, he is here,—he has written a great novel, a great poem, or what not." We are put on the *qui vive,* and by and bye when the poor little puffed out product struts upon the stage we find that he belongs to the ephemera. These strains are common. We watch anxiously for the pool to move that we may be healed of these grotesque vagaries of mental disease. We gaze longingly up the road for a rescuer and see but wind-piled columns of choking dust.

We comfort ourselves a little with Kipling; and Besant and Black are still with us, but we sigh to be healed of Hardy's decadence, and of the tastelessness of *The Martian,*—poor withered fruit of DuMaurier's dotage.

We cry out for something in place of this dry rot, this attenuated intellectuality; this vain struggling after startling effects. Our sensibilities are mangled and scarified day by day by the rude contact of a crowd of weird, grotesque, figures who flit their fantastic way across the stage.

We are surrounded by writers of queer distorted verse, drunken with their own turgid, muddy, rhetoric; dancing fauns and satyrs holding revels over social uncleanness like crows over carrion; dreamers of meaningless visions, makers of verse full of incomprehensible gibberish. Are they of healthy human kind who beat time in this rout? Is that young woman who writes tigerish verses of a tigerish passion, all the Sappho we shall have? Must we call a plain case of erotic mania, poetic fervour? Is that jingler of little verselets, that journeyman carver of odd forms of speech, to be our Tennyson? Shall we force ourselves to see deathless harmony in a mere mush of words, simply because it is labeled poetry? Must we give *Jude The Obscure* and *The Martian* a place with

Vanity Fair and *David Copperfield?* We "have been tolled by holy bell to church, have sat at good men's feasts," and we cannot forget those feasts. If there is nothing else, give us some good stories of bears and tigers, of jungles, of far-off lands where men are breathing free, and where there is good wholesome blood-letting and killing.

Thus the Pessimist.

But we may be comforted in a measure; we have our blessings and must not be unmindful of them. Into this world where everything is worn out and steeped in the ditch-water of dullness, comes an interrogation point of a man,—Andrew Lang. If needs be, he will smash every idol and question every fad. Let the fashions change as they will, here is a man who clings to the verities of truth and mental good health.

He is cool-blooded and temperate

when others are furious. He retains his composure amidst the clamours of little coteries of intellectual starvelings frantically admiring each other and bound to coerce all others into a like service. Into this market-place of small wares, Lang comes as the Sealer of Weights and Measures. He hears unmoved the dingdonging of the auction bell, the selling of names. He cannot be hypnotized by the posturings and caperings of literary mountebanks. Over the Kingdom of Fools, he is the upright and just judge, with plenary jurisdiction.

Many idols, some false and some true, have been ranged before this judgment seat. Along with other stucco-work, is poor old Poet Bailey, the solace and comfort of our grandmothers. Look in your *Poets Argosy* or *Gems of Poetry,* and you will unearth among other ancient treasures, "O no, we never mention her," and like lollipops and sweet things from Bailey. I knew Bailey first, through the melancholia of my friend Mr. Richard Swiveller, who turned from the perfidious Sophy to Bailey's soothing charm. I learned Bailey better through Lang, who treated his reputation charitably, bestowing only a spanking,—lightly laid on. In fact Lang thinks that Bailey might have been something of a poet, he pleased so many simple folk. In this genial fashion does he judge all small sinners.

But when Lang reads the bead-roll of genius, names that were before heard and forgotten stick like burrs. They stand for something. The dead heroes walk again in new-kindled light. Bunyan, and Montaigne, and Scott, and all great and noble souls gain new nobility and pass unscathed through that wise and kindly judgment. Lang has the grand hailing sign and password of the kinship of genius. He recognizes his fellows for what they are across the centuries and the wide seas.

Thus it is that he flashed recognition over to Holmes and Lowell, of all Americans the most like himself. He discovered Kipling in the wilderness of India, and gave him a passport into the World of Letters. And now Kipling has become the man of three continents, with fame enough to fill them all.

Lang is best as a critic and hero-worshipper. He and Nordau are almost the only ones left to police our world of literary nondescripts. Carlyle, that harsh block of Scottish granite is gone, and humbug and cant may thrive apace. Thackeray, Keeper of a House for the Correction of Snobs, stalks his grim beat no more. Macaulay, who so deftly put Mr. Robert Montgomery in the pillory, is with the dust of the earth. Dr. Holmes, vested with large jurisdiction over vulgar pretenders in these American Colonies, has no further judgments to execute. There are no more. Gallant spirits, loyal to the truth, when shall we look upon your like again! You yet have some security that your work will be carried on, for Lang is your living disciple. You may be sure that some frothy cant will be sponged out; some humbugs will be dosed heroically; some literary reputations will be put in the stocks where we may all have our fling at them. Who shall say that these labors have been in vain? The snobs did not run about at ease while Thackeray was at them. Some of them were killed and some cured.

Where, for instance is the Fashionable Authoress,—where is Lady Fanny Flummery? She was done to death by Thackeray, and has left no heirs. I believe that Lang claims he had a commission once to discover the habitat of her successor, but was compelled to make return of the same unsatisfied. It is true, Thackeray was not always so successful. He tried to suppress the poet who writes Odes to Dying Things, such as Frogs, Brook Trout, or whatever it may be, but he could not do it. She,—I use the feminine advisedly—is immortal; suppress her in one generation and she will break out in the next. She still lives to infest the watches of the moon, to write Odes and other nameless things. She was a Miss Bunion in Thackeray's time and averred that her youth resembled:

A violet shrinking meanly
When blows the March wind keenly;
A timid fawn on upland lawn,
Where oak-boughs rustle greenly.

These thrice-crazed ones scatter sweet flowers about us still. Their dainty ribbon-tied volumes strew our libraries like autumn leaves in Vallombrosa. Yet after all, Thackeray's punishment of Miss Bunion was not in vain. His magisterial process is still out against her successors. Nor was it a vain labor for Mr. Yellowplush and the Sallybrated Mr. Smith, over a cold hoyster in the Yellowplush pantry, to hale Mr. Bulwer Lytton to the torture. That day was Fine Writing punctured so that the sawdust padding ran out of it.

Unlike Nordau, Lang is not a Tartar of savage severity toward his convicts. That Vidocq of continental letters hangs his victims in chains, in barbaric style, for the sun and wind to bleach. In this he is like Carlyle, who had a troglodyte nature and brained *his* with a stone axe. Lang has an Englishman's love of fair play. He gives quarter and treats his victim with courtly grace during the necessary torture. Captain John Smith did not behead the three Turks before the walls of Regall with more blandness or gentle affability.

Lang makes the desert places of scholarship, fair and pleasant with beauty and verdure. Greek is dry and arid when taught by dusty-brained pedantic parrots. Lang transmutes it until it lives again, bringing forth boughs like a plant. In his interpretation its dreary tasks become pleasant pastimes. He would have the college dry-as-dusts give way for one greater than they,—the deathless singer, the sightless poet who saw all things; who found the Soul of Song in far off mystic Illium, in surging seas and on battle fields, on dreary ocean coasts and lonely lost lands, in the tombs of the dead and in the darkness beyond, in the loves and hopes of statesmen and warriors, of rustics and ploughmen round their hearth-fires, in the legends of a thousand years, in the wanderings of the Grecian Chieftan and his return to the great hall where the suitors met; who could pluck his dearest thought from the welcome home which the dumb and faithful Argus gave the wanderer. Lang would have the ardent student follow Ulysses in his wanderings unbelittled by translators until by and bye the splendour and power of that wonderful melody would not let him sleep. Soon a knowledge of Greek would come, but better than this would come a knowledge of Homer. The finest thing in Lang is his worship of Homer. He seems to continually hunger and thrist for him. He holds him close to his heart in half-boyish adoration and fervour. He is a jealous lover and cannot bear that Pope and Morris and others of the translator's mob should put Homer into their rhyming strait-jackets. He is savage upon their trespasses and punishes them with many stinging scoffs and gibes. He has lived so much with Homer, that at will the centuries roll back and he sees the world that Homer saw. He loves Homer's lightest word better than all of Pope's stilted rhymes. He makes one mourn for his ignorance of Greek, for it means that he can never know Homer for all that he is.

Lang has the advantage of being a Scotchman with English advantages. He is a later Socrates in a dress coat. Some one has said that he is too finished a product to become popular with the mass. I will admit that he is neither dull and heavy nor light and vulgar. After his title page there is not a dull line, and even a title page with the name of Andrew Lang on it will illuminate a whole library. When I find a library tenanted by Andrew Lang, I confess to feeling vastly increased respect for the proprietor. Even the presence of *She,* or of *Mr. Barnes of New York,* in that library, cannot entirely destroy this good opinion. The scholar and man of letters may, by inadvertence, become the victim of the brazen train-boy.

Lang disdains fine writing, and yet always writes finely, with the virile powerful touch of a master. He does not hold himself above the common speech of people if by ranging there he can find the apt word or the rightly turned phrase. A scholar with the art to conceal the mere repelling externals of scholarship, Yale or Oxford could not take the fine temper out of such a soul as his. He did not come forth from the pedagogic inquisition afflicted with intellectual rickets. Whether the University Procrustes found him too long or too short, cannot be discovered from any tokens he bears. He comes into a world of much fustian scholarship, a true scholar, a loyal perfect knight of the pen.

But Lang is not all the critic, not all the man of war,—the knight whose keen and biting rapier plays like lightning among the false and the foolish.

There is another Lang,—a poet and hero-worshipper, a lover of homely things, of homely human-kind; one who takes content in watching his peaches ripen on the wall and his grapes on their trellis; one who loves walks of peace and quietness, and who can see the "splendour in the grass, the glory in the flower;" one who can look upon lovers strolling together in the sweet English May-time with kindly eyes and softened heart. He is no longer young, but he can remember the loves and hopes of youth. With him,—

"Manhood's noonday shadows hold
The dews of boyhood's morning."

If this were not so he could not have written such verses of baffling sweetness as these;—

> Who wins his love shall lose her;
> Who loses her shall gain;
> For still the spirit wooes her,
> A soul without a stain;
> And mem'ry still pursues her,
> With longings not in vain.
>
> *   *   *
>
> In dreams she grows not older,
> The land of dreams among,
> Though all the world wax colder
> Though all the songs be sung;
> In dreams shall he behold her,
> Still fair, and kind, and young.

HONORE DE BALZAC

As Balzac is favored with a minor place in Max Nordau's Gallery of Degenerates, I am disposed to make a deprecatory bow to that eminent vivisectionist.

Some characters should be described by describing their opposites—Mr. Gulliver said that he could better realize the huge dimensions of the Brobdingnaggians, because of his recent experiences in Lilliput.

If I shall take liberties of comparison with any of the idols in our home temple of fame, it is not to make them seem more diminutive, but to give a better perspective for Balzac. Few of our countrymen have broken into his prodigious storehouse. The charming insularity of the truly patriotic American, prejudices him against the products of the effete despotisms. He says, we have our own shrines, why go abroad to worship?

Hence the elevation of Howells, who never says damn, and who never levels even a small corner of his faithful kodac on any of the tabooed vulgarities. I confess I prefer a somewhat coarse bluntness to this chaste veiling. I defy any one, for instance, to tell just what sins Howells intends to impute to Bartley Hubbard. If Balzac had dealt with him, he would have stripped his soul naked, even if it did take coarse and vulgar words to do it.

As we progress in social development, our society grows more clubbish.

Gentle woman organizes herself, and pursues and gluts herself on Culture, without ceasing. We have Arnold Clubs and Browning Clubs, and what not, and the stones of Rome and the number of bricks in St. Paul's must be counted in didactic essay. Culture does not have much chance to escape these indefatigable pursuers. Yet those who grow weary of this child's game of Culture, this fishing in a water-pail and drawing nothing up, can find easy relief in the wisdom and strength of Balzac.

Why watch continually the never-moving waters of smug literary mediocrity, when you have only to climb the steeps a little way and look upon the mighty sea? This immortal genius can bide its time however. It may yet become the fad of the Culture Clubs; a reigning mode in literature.

The *Lily of The Valley,* or *Ursula,* of crystal purity, may yet fill the place of the highly immoral *Trilby*. Père Goriot, may supersede Howell's Broomfield Corey, or that delightful old philistine, who gained ephemeral riches in mineral paint.

We assure those who have become accustomed to the pure and elevated morality of Ella Wheeler Wilcox, and *The Quick and the Dead,* that they will find nothing to shock or disturb them in Balzac. The austere virgin, Propriety, should also be warned that she will see nothing very offensive in Balzac and that she had better not take the trouble to look for it. If she should by any chance have breathed too long the mephitic sewer gas of the Erotic School of American Fiction and Poetry, she may not at first have free respiration in the higher altitudes of Balzac.

It is true that he does not aim to have a moral, ticketed and labeled as such, for every tale. He paints human life as he finds it, in its baseness and glory, in its weakness and its strength.

He does not announce the moral, yet it is always present; in the punishment and repentance of the wicked, in the lives of the pure in heart, and in the hells which evil souls build for themselves.

Our gentle E. P. Roe, who should be called Pencils-and-Pickles, he is so much affected by young women towards the end of their bread-and-butter age, always builds his moral first, and then fits his story to it afterwards. He carries his pulpit around on his back as a snail does its residence, or an organ-grinder his instrument of torture and if he gets half a chance he will set it up and preach.

Balzac tells his story and lets the moral take care of itself. He has no patent theological-seminary plan for converting sinners. Where is there a finer sermon than the conversion of Doctor Minoret, led to repentance by the child he loved.

"Can it be that you believe in God?" she cried with artless joy, letting fall the tears that gathered in her eyes.

* * *

"My God," he said in a trembling voice, raising his head, "if any one can obtain my pardon and lead me to Thee, surely it is this spotless creature. Have mercy on the repentant old age that this poor child presents to Thee."

Balzac has the carelessness and abandon of conscious power. He plays the prodigal with his talents. The sweepings of his attic would stock a dozen common skulls with genius, and make a dozen latter-day reputations. He is not concerned with the petty fears and alarms of small minds. One of their gods is Brevity. Your writer of magazine novelettes; your mere parlour entertainer, affects to abhor the Superfluous Word.

Balzac never bothers his head about it. His words come in great torrents, and the excess cannot hide his kingly port. Always present is the dramatic quality. You watch with terror for his next effect. Our colder Teutonic blood has too little of this fire, and so genius becomes atrophied and lifeless. Afraid to give Nature speech, our strugglers after fame belittle the passions and make them tame and commonplace, or paint them in strange bizarre colors and in mangled grotesqueness. How different the mighty genius of Balzac! When Doctor Minoret weeps, Balzac says:—

The tears of old men are as terrible as those of children are natural.

The sorrows of Père Goriot have a thousand eloquent tongues. What a profound and immeasurable baseness is that which robbed him of his peace.

Throned in the majesty of death his whispers are heartrending. Sometimes he babbles childish nonsense, and sometimes shrieks his last terrible resentments. He calls for his daughters alternately in curses and words of endearment. You can feel him groping through the thick shadows for them, but they do not come. It is King Lear, with a difference. Finally, in the moment of dissolution, God is merciful to this shattered soul. He sees again his daughters as little children, and calls them by the childish names he once gave them; and so he passes from this inhuman world.

One must walk with Balzac in fear and dread. His are not always the pleasant tasks of an idle hour. He will lead you through the hell of the living where you will meet dreadful shades and weeping, crucified, souls. He will also show you complacent Respectability sitting in placid ease, "storing yearly little dues of wheat and wine and oil." He preaches a thousand sermons of the erring majesty of human life, but he does not, like Zola, batten on dunghills, and show you how much muck he can dig up.

And now, what is the main difference between him and the Lilliputians?

They are mere photographers, taking machine pictures with painful care. It is the difference between a kodac and the brush of a great master.

He may be ever so careless and slovenly, but he has the hand of power and when he sweeps his brush across the canvass, that canvass becomes one of the dear and priceless treasures of the world through all the centuries.

WILLIAM MAKEPEACE THACKERAY

Captious persons may insist that they be made acquainted with the authority which prompts this further presentation of Thackeray lore.

This seems to be agreeable to the demand that the distant suburbs of culture shall remain in eternal calm, except for the harryings of the Chatauqua Course and the literary tea and toast of the culture clubs. Yet this message will be unpretending as becomes one from a place so far distant from the habitat of learned and approved reviewers. The point of view at least should not unduly prejudice the relation, for the ferment of London, Boston and New York is busy upon newer themes, and the soil once worked to exhaustion now lies fallow.

Not consenting to the paramount jurisdiction of any reviewer whosoever, there is here presented some cumulative testimony on Thackeray, for it is the duty of each generation to testify to all that has aforetime been done in letters. Thus divers testimonies can be preserved for the use of posterity when it shall make up its final verdict. This review is offered by one who loves his task, a witness on minor points, merely as a deposition *in rei perpetua memoriam*, for what even such an one has thought of Thackeray may become a matter of curious and valuable interest some hundreds of years hence. The toiler and dreamer must look to that final judgment, and not the applause of the easily satisfied, who may crown a favorite to-day and uncrown him to-morrow.

Not in profane analogy to the final judgment in the moral and spiritual world, but in the conceit of an idle hour, one can imagine a court of last resort for authors in which there shall be a final decree on all fames and reputations; where worth and not names shall control; where even some rejected manuscripts will give their testimony not disqualified by any past editorial verdict; where some obscure poets shall have due commendation, and the swollen reputations of some great men will suffer proper diminution. The poor scholar who has escaped prosperity shall there be crowned with the tardy bays, and many darkened garrets of our Grub Streets will become visibly glorious in that effulgent justice. The magazine magnate who hears not the voice of genius until it be properly advertised, and who has spent his life-time putting its inspirations into strait-jackets; the Professional Organizer of Clacques for Small Performers; the Critics Banditti who hold up all travelers on the road to fame, will, let us trust, on that last judgment day find their deserved place among the goats. But surely there are some fames that will grow brighter and brighter in that last winnowing. Unless the known standards of excellence shall fail, in all the world of nineteenth century authorship, Thackeray will be given first place.

Sometimes, owing to the failing memories of men, priceless things are lost sight of for a time, yet assurance seems now so full that it cannot be so with Thackeray. With him, however, more than with any other author, the effect he produced on his readers forms a curious study. Some minds instinctively dislike him and yet delight in Dickens and Bulwer Lytton. Such soils, however well sown with Thackerayism, blossom only into the meagerest appreciation. This trait is like unto the fabled inability of the North Briton to comprehend a joke. Is it because the satire of Thackeray is so sweeping and all-embracing that even the most obtuse reader imagines he is being mocked at and that all of his own vanities and follies are being rudely caricatured before his eyes? Happy is the man who can laugh at his own follies and jest at himself for the fool that he was on yesterday. To him Thackeray is a well-spring of delight.

Both the comedy and tragedy of life have a sameness from generation to generation. It is a common place to say that names and social customs and forms of government change, but the nature of man remains as it was, and that the creations of Molière and Shakespeare will always have living duplicates. Who has not known a Tartuffe? Even a Falstaff is not difficult to find, and as for Nym, Pistol and Bardolph, they are as common as sawdust saloons.

I have met the Old Campaigner,— busy breeder of divorces that she is, and Becky Sharp still lives and continues to shoot young curates, and other impressionable males, dead with her soft glances.

On the very threshold of Thackeray's world one cannot help but linger a little over his endearing personal qualities. Soon he will show us life's baseness and meanness, and it seems good to pause over some happier things before launching into the blacker and deeper currents. He was one of the lovable men of literature. Count them up and you will see how few of these there are. Some of the greatest names stand for icebergs of personality, and you can feel the lowering temperature as you near them. Do you always love the man behind the book? It is rank treason to suggest it but can you feel affection for the man Dickens, for the man Tennyson, or for Bulwer Lytton? I confess that I cannot; they are only graven images and mere makers of books, as remotely frigid as the north pole. There is some coldness in the blood accounting for this that cannot be explained or analyzed. But, what warmth and cheer and glow of good fellowship and kindliness radiates from Thackeray and Lamb and Holmes. When you read their words they become alive again, and when you think of them as dead, it brings a sharp pang of grief; a sense of personal loss. Time cannot still their heart throbs, and life and love are pulsing yet, despite the tokens of mortality.

It may be that this repellant coolness in Tennyson and Dickens is due to the drop of Semitic blood ascribed to them by anthropoligical investigators. I think it is Besant who says that this tincture of the elder race is neccessary to mental perfection, and that where it comes it leavens with an added genius the tough stubborn fibre of the Teutonic intellect. He adds that we all need a little of it in order to properly ripen our talents.

In the lesser memoirs of the great poet we read that after he had written *The Revenge* and commited it to his publisher's hands and before it had become public property, he invited a choice company to hear it read. Probably no one but he could bring together such a group of listeners within the four seas. His grave biographer describes his reading generally as a "mysterious incantation exceedingly impressive," and as he read on towards the end every heart was awed by the wonderful power of the immortal poem.

He finally came to the close with such a strange mixture of genius and thrift that his hearers were frozen lifeless:—

And they mann'd the Revenge with a swarthier alien crew,
And away she sail'd with her loss and long'd for her own;
When a wind from the lands they had ruin'd awoke from sleep
And the water began to heave and the weather to moan,
And or ever that evening ended a great gale blew,
And a wave like the wave that is raised by an earthquake grew,
Till it smote on their hulls and their sails and their masts and their flags,
And the whole sea plunged and fell on the shot-shatter'd navy of Spain,

>And the little Revenge herself went down
>   by the island crags
>To be lost evermore in the main,
>   and the beggars only gave me three
>   hundred pounds for it—"

Quoth my Lord Tennyson, not making pause at all between the last words of the poem and his execrations on the hard-hearted publishers who had driven a close bargain with him. It is hard to have the deathless minstrel sweep one hand across his harp, while with the other he clinks and counts his guineas. Doubtless not one of that noble assemblage ever forgot the scene, or could ever look on *Locksley Hall* as anything but a commercial pot-boiler, or on *In Memoriam* as other than a task to be paid for at so much a line.

Behind the scenes one sees dimly the publishers and the poet, driving the bargains of an old clothes shop.

How different this from Dante who "could hold heart-break at bay for twenty years and not let himself die until his task was done," or Lamb "winning his way, with sad and patient soul, through evil and pain, and strange calamity." These two marshalled life's forces through black shadows, the one with a warrior's stern, set, face, that never lightened and the other with pleasant jest, heedless of whether he won or lost, so he but hid the heartache. Who could turn from this real tragedy to Byron's counterfeit, or feel affection for him in his theatrical sorrow as he displayed in many postures his many times broken heart to the public gaze?

It is for him who is a man first and a genius afterwards, that we reserve our best affection. We accord this to Thackeray for he had the heart of a child that worldly wisdom could not spoil.

It is a far leap from these thoughts to Thackeray's land of snobs. He is markedly eminent as the only great specialist on this subject. He has taken them apart and put them together, and reduced them to their original elements. He has admired, dissected and played with them, and artfully drawn them out and felinely leaped upon them from cunning concealments. He has dug and searched for snobs in all social formations, and never without reward. He has made scientific research into all kinds, qualities, conditions and degrees of snobs, and classified, arranged, named, numbered, indexed and cross-referenced them. He has grilled them, sometimes savagely, and sometimes lovingly, for he had a grotesque form of affection for them such as Dickens said that he had for the pigs which he saw disporting themselves in the streets of New York. Given one scale of any species of snob, and Thackeray could construct the complete animal. He takes a just pride in his cabinet of snobs where there are multitudes of them artistically arranged with pens stuck through their snobbish thoraxes. Among these remains are Clerical, Royal, Military, Respectable, Great, City, Banking, Scholastic, Irish, Sporting, University, Theatrical, Professional and Official Snobs. Being pressed to define Literary Snobs, the satirical rogue says:—

The fact is that in the literary profession there are no snobs. Look around over the whole body of British men of letters, and I defy you to point out a single instance of vulgarity, or envy, or assumption.

This genial snob-hunter sometimes beats up his own thickets. He admits that he would rather walk down Pall Mall arm in arm with a Lord than with a commoner, and would feel a snobbish elation if he could only be seen between two dukes in Picadilly. In the divine ardour of the chase he is willing to jeeringly trice himself up. If at any time one feels a tendency to snobbishness, he can de-snobize himself by consulting Thackeray's probe and scalpel. We arise from this feast of snobs to ask if there is any place free from the Snob? Is there no wild of England, Scotland or Ireland, or Thibet or Crim-Tartary, or among the Anthroppopphaghi, where a snob is not?

Thackeray never gave but the most casual investigation to the fauna of this continent. He had doubtless read our history and knew that there were no snobs here, and that in this republic all men were created equal and recognized neither rank nor social condition as conferring any distinction. He must have found that snobs, like weeds, do not grow on new soils. No, we do not love a lord better than a commoner; we do not envy our neighbours; we do not think meanly of and inflict slights on those less fortunate than ourselves; we do not think better of any man because of his wealth. No one here "meanly admires mean things," which is his definition of a snob. Our international marriages with foreign titles have been possible only because of the singular worth of the groom involved, and,—also by reason of the worth of the bride.

With us, kind hearts are more than coronets, and, thank heaven, we have a proper contempt for the social sycophancy of the degenerate Briton. Those fecund Irish kings and noble families of the three islands have no noble descendants here who brag of their long descent, and we who know that our ancestry is noble, never mention it and do not esteem ourselves for it.

There is one line of fiction in which Thackeray is not great. He portrayed no murderers, no Napoleonic criminals who slept in the contriving of crime and awoke to do it. He had no love for slumming, and did not, like a respectable sort of scavenger, rake over the refuse of the London streets for lessons and sermons and fine morals with which to adorn his romance.

He made the novel a public conveyance where all sorts of people might find carriage; where Parson Honeyman is rudely jostled by Mr. Moss, and the gentle Amelia and Captain Raff touch elbows; where callow Pendennis hotly courts the ancient Fotheringay, chaperoned by the redoubtable Costigan; where Becky Sharp and her vis-a-vis, the stately Semiramis Pinkerton, picked up as the coach rolls by Chiswick Mall, make faces at each other; where the Castlewoods cease not their genteel family quarrels, and Lady Maria begins that little Affair with the French dancing master; where the Virginians arrange for the early morning meeting with their lately esteemed friend, G. W.; where Philip glowers hatred at his father, and Clive and Barnes Newcome fall to cousinly insults and blows; while ever watchful in his corner sits a humorous "Literary Gent," as the genial Harry Foker calls him, taking notes and chuckling now and then as the coach speeds away, and the ruts bring out the temper of the passengers.

There are inns to be made, and new passengers to be taken up, and old ones to be put down, and country roads stretching before, and narrow towns to pass, and by and by, the din and roar of the great Babylon. But the journey is never long and never weary for always you are keeping close company with human life, and are looking breathlessly into its meanness and its majesty.

Take joy of this ferment and turmoil of living and loving and hating, and so that you may love it the more heartily, turn and look upon the single-seated equipages of romance that are trundled before us in this part of the world. The single nondescript passenger that you see is the author's fad in morals, religion or politics, or some flotsam gleaned from the nine days talk of the tea parties, or furbished out of the last labor strike, the newest phase of the New Woman, the Chicago Fire, the Charleston Earthquake, or the last visitation of Cholera or Yellow Fever. Any commonplace of this kind furnishes plot and pabulum and all manner of excellencies to our story-writers of pauperized wits. Among them are the Obituary Novelists, who, like the Obituary Poets in the country newspapers, go hand in hand with Death. Let Death come to a city with generous stroke, in Flood, Fire, Earthquake, or Plague and the public can draw at ninety days on the Obituary Novelists for this mortuary aftermath of fiction. Thus comes our Dreary School of Romance.

Its upbuilders select a supposed dramatic situation or center and round it range the puppet characters, who chatter from page to page some text of commonplace and are as sentient and alive as a lot of wooden Indians. Thus we have had; "Bulwarks Burned Down," "The Earth Shook," "Saved by the Flood," "Plague Stricken," etc., etc. "The Washerwoman of Finchley Common," would be of riotous interest as compared with some of these. Their admirers are one with the Exeter Hall enthusiast who declared that he would rather be the author of the tract named than of *Paradise Lost*.

But come away to where we have better metal. Thackeray deals with respectable wickedness in the main; a wickedness of cushioned pews and pretty pulpits, and eminently virtuous drawing rooms; of assemblies where highly respectable people such as you and I know, eat, drink and make merry; a wickedness of pleasant family circles where all hands quarrel in a perfectly genteel way; a wickedness which goes hand in hand with Christian church-going, with Christian alms-giving, with loyal support of the State and all established institutions; a wickedness which dresses in the paint and tinsel of conventional moralities, which sits in the boxes in Vanity Fair, and looks down with stern scorn on the ungenteel low-down wickedness of the pit;—in short a philistine, pharisaical, canting, time-serving, toadying, sham-loving, holierthan-thou wickedness that cankers and rots character like a leprosy. You will sometimes turn your head away from this rout of respectable sinners for shame of our common humanity.

You do not need to pray to be saved from the crimes of the statute books, but you may need to be saved from the sins of the Old Campaigner, of Mrs. Bute Crawley, of Barnes Newcome, of Old Osborne, of Lady Kew, and the Reverend Honeyman, of the Pontos, the Botibels, the Clutterbucks, and Lady Susan Scraper, and many others. These were all of approved respectability and some of them made a great figure in Vanity Fair. They did not pick pockets or commit murder, but acted in all things as a great many respectable people about you do, yet how you despise and loathe them. These are Thackeray's Helots, drunken with greed and selfishness and all uncharitableness, shown as examples of what respectable men and women may do and still keep their rags of respectability.

We do not have to be warned against the wickedness of Sykes, and Fagin, and Jonas Chuzzlewit, of Quilp and Brass. Their depravity has no enticement; it is vulgar and repellant. The warning in Thackeray's sermons is for the Respectable Wicked, and the most complacent sinner will wince under this lash. Thackeray loved a man, and would have nothing less. With him:—

> One ruddy drop of manly blood
> The surging sea outweighs.

He never spares himself. Here is one of his self-indictments.

> I never could count how many causes went to produce any given effect in a person's life, and have been, for my own part many a time quite misled in my own case, fancying some grand, some magnanimous, some virtuous reason for an

act of which I was proud, when lo! some pert little satirical monitor springs up inwardly, upsetting the fond humbug which I was cherishing—the peacock's tail wherein my absurd vanity had clad itself—and says; "Away with boasting; I am the cause of your virtue my lad. You are pleased that yesterday at dinner you refrained from the dry champagne. My name is Worldly Prudence, not Self Denial, and I caused you to refrain. You are pleased because you gave a guinea to Diddler. I am Laziness, not Generosity which inspired you. You hug yourself because you resisted other temptation? Coward, it was because you dared not run the risk of the wrong! Out with your peacock's plumage! Walk off in the feathers which Nature gave you, and thank Heaven they are not altogether black."

Yet the same hand wrote this of a woman looking back forty

years to the love of her youth:—

Oh, what tears have they shed, gentle eyes! Oh, what faith has it kept, tender heart! If love lives through all life, and survives through all sorrow; and remains steadfast with us through all changes; and in all darkness of spirit burns brightly; and, if we die, deplores us forever, and loves still equally; and exists with the very last gasp and throb of the faithful bosom—whence it passes with the pure soul beyond death; sure it shall be immortal.

And like it is what he said of the gulf of time, and parting, and grief.—

And the past and its dear histories, and youth and its hopes and passions, and tones and looks forever echoing in the heart, and present in the memory—these no doubt, poor Clive saw and heard as he looked across the great gulf of time, and parting, and grief, and beheld the woman he had loved for many years. There she sits; the same, but changed; as gone from him as if she were dead; departed indeed into another sphere, and into a kind of death.

If Thackeray dearly loved a man, he also loved a boy. He is the historian, the epic poet of boyhood. The boy is an unknown quantity to the average novelist; he is elusive and protean and evades description. Some great novelists, although undoubtedly once boys themselves, make mere caricatures of boys. Little Lord Fauntelroy was a charming creature but he was not a boy. D'Israeli's boys are all old men; they attain threescore before they are twenty. Witness the grand entrance of some of these unfeathered ones in the world of politics and letters. They discourse of affairs of state before they have achieved the big manly voice. If you should chance to meet one of these very old young gentlemen at Rodwell Regis or Dr. Birch's school you would no more think of giving him a tip to buy sweets with, than you would of tipping Mr. Gladstone. Thomas Bailey Aldrich and Mark Twain have told us of some real boys, and William Allen White is now engaged, as I understand, in the restoration of the Boy, to fiction.

In behalf of these gentlemen and all men who have been boys I protest against expurgated editions of boyhood. Like Cromwell with the portrait painter, I want to have the picture show all the blemishes. You will have to make long search in Dickens before you will find a real boy. He has some impossible creations that are called boys, but as a rule they are grotesque freaks, mere caricatures, made up by selecting and emphasizing some one boyish trait. This gives a mere fragment of a boy. The Fat Boy for instance, simply eats and sleeps,—admittedly too meager an endowment of boyish talent.

The Dickens Boy is given to the most impossible grown-up language. Here is a sample from Mrs. Lirriper's Lodgings. The boy says, in a burst of childish confidence to the old lady who has adopted him.—

And now dear Gran. let me kneel down here, where I have been used to say my prayers, and let me fold my face for just a minute in your gown, and let me cry, for you have been more than mother, more than father, more than sisters, friends to me.

This is exactly the way the forty-year-old boy talks in a popular play. But no real ten-year-old ever talked like that. Oliver Twist was not much of a boy. The nearest he came to it, was when he asked for more, and when he blacked Noah Claypole's eye. But these events seemed in the nature of accidents and not indicative of any settled boyish habit.

Thackeray has no counterfeit boys. He never got over being a boy himself and so he knew boys. He does not have them continually at stage business. They fight and fag each other and are flogged religiously and unavailingly; they fill up on hardbake and raspberry tart, they run in debt for goodies, and dote on hampers from home, and hate books and love fun. Clive goes to Aunt Honeyman's and she stuffs him with sweets as is the manner of aunts the world over. Sad is the childhood that does not have such an aunt. I vow I would rather have seen the fight between Champion Major the First Cock of Doctor Birch's School, and the Tutbury Pet, or the one between Cuff and Dobbin, than the combat between the late Messrs Fitzsimmons and Corbett.

But Thackeray is most happy with his boys in the salad time, between hay and grass, when the childish treble changes to a more virile note. Few elders understand a boy at this time, nor does he understand himself. If you choose to laugh at the many nebulous aspirations, hopes and ambitions that come to him, then you are laughing over the grave of your own youth where lies all that was best in you. Make your mirth kindly, for so you toiled, and sorrowed and played up the slope of manhood. The silly hours, the follies in love, the wanton freaks and callow vices, the fitful starts that mark the changing mind, are all pictures of your own youth. You have turned them to the wall and forgotten them, or wish you could forget them. Thackeray has dealt kindly with this world of hobbledehoyhood. He has peopled it with Arthur Pendennis, Phillip, Clive, the Virginians and many more of unripe wits. He is youth's kindliest, most generous mentor. 'Tis sometimes one whether this boy-man is laughing or crying over this dreamland of youth.

It was as if he had the same opinion of Dr. Busby, who was asked how he contrived to keep all his preferments, and the head-mastership of Westminister School, through the turbulent times of Charles I, Cromwell, and Charles II; He replied:—"The fathers govern the nation; the mothers govern the fathers; the boys govern the mothers; and I govern the boys."

He could live over again that many-sided boyhood with its selfishness and generosity, its cruelty and humanity, its justice and injustice, its queer, strange, code of established laws and customs. Always a boy at heart, he could easily turn back to the old days of smiles and tears, of feasting and fighting, of loosely mingled work and play, and feel again the thrill of those early griefs and joys, and that first fond love for many companions whom the dust has long covered.

It was in child-hearted mood that he wrote the poem where are these lines.—

> I'd say we suffer and we strive
> Not less or more as men than boys;
> With grizzled beards at forty-five,
> As erst at twelve in corduroys.
> And if in time of sacred youth,
> We learned at home to love and pray,
> Pray heaven that early love and truth
> May never wholly pass away.

The Thackeray Woman is a delicate subject—a complex creature, and not to be roughly classified. Our author has been widely accused of making his women either fools or knaves, and of disparaging the sex to the point of slander. This criticism is really based on supersensitive gallantry. In fact, Thackeray treated the sexes impartially, and dealt out stripes and favor with an equal hand.

He did not create any lofty and flawless women, but neither did he create any men of this character.

Becky Sharpe, The Old Campaigner, and the fair false Beatrix and many other selfish, nagging, toadying, respectable and semi-respectable women that he has painted are in his Rogues' Gallery, side by side with George Osborne, the brainless cad, the Marquis of Steyne, and Barnes Newcome.

We are not unmindful that Zenobia Packer, who belongs to no one knows how many clubs, and is president of the Woman's Emancipation League, and who aims a rapid fire of treatises and addresses at the Tyrant, Man, and is high chum with Lady Summersault, the English Head of the Movement for Purity and Reform, thinks that Amelia Sedley was a little fool, and that all of the Thackeray women of gentle mould who prayed among their children, and clung fiercely to their household deities, and never cared whether they had any rights or not, were poor puling weak-spirited creatures, who would be entirely out of date now.

Go thy way, Zenobia, to thy clubs and thy culture, and thy meat for the strong-minded; pace the platform with mannish strides; harangue obdurate Man until he cries for quarter, and hunt the bubble Notoriety from convention to convention.

Tyrant Man would return your compliments with interest if he dared. And you, Hysterical One who spleen on marriage service lest it have occult power to subjugate you, and who analyze and re-analyze all your emotions and feelings before you use them, and hold high prate and debate over *deum* and *teum,* follow your labyrinth and let petty Discontent gnaw you, but leave healthy humanity to its worship of old-fashioned idols.

If to be gentle, and loving, and kindly, and unselfish; to be ignorant of most of the wickedness of the world, to believe in and trust and idealize a faulty, human, son or brother or husband, and to forgive him seventy times seven, and to pour unmeasured love upon him without pausing to see whether it is all measured back or not; to be generous and charitable to all erring souls, and to hate all wickedness, stamps a woman as a poor weak-spirited creature, then may heaven send us more of such women to bless and cheer the world and make it better. Amelia, it is true, loved a cad, but evil tongues were hushed in her presence. The Little Sister artlessly dropped her h's, and said "feller," and was not at all strong-minded, but in silence she let her own good name suffer a deadly wound in order that she might save the boy, not her own, from an inheritance of shame.

Some apology is due for approaching the everlasting parallel between Dickens and Thackeray; but this habit of comparison has become a fixed and ineradicable trait in all of their admirers. The question of superiority between them is probably as unworthy of serious contention as are some of those favorites of the Ethopian debating societies.

Dickens will undoubtedly always be more popular with the masses. His humor, his mannerisms, his bent for fine writing, his long drawn pathos, his unwearying play of sorrow and emotion and his conventional sermonizing on the moralities, are more taking than the quick, sweeping strokes of Thackeray.

Thackeray disdained pretentious writing and all overdrawn, overworn scenes. He has no Solitary Horsemen, no prefatory tales of wind and storm, no stale theatrical tricks or devices, or tawdry stage properties. He leaves all the gorgeous imagery of sky and storm and landscape to other limners. Life's great joys and sorrows are not made wearying with long speech or ornate funeral rhetoric. Before a death bed, he is not like Dame Quickly or some garrulous caretaker of the chamber, chattering and gossipping of the last hour; he but reverently draws the curtain back for a momentary view and then closes it again. He does not prologue his art and bid you prepare to laugh or weep before the occasion.

Yet he excels Dickens, and, indeed, most others, as a masters of style. The pedant, the mere grammarian, or linguistic martinet, prunes and pares our mother-tongue into bashful regularity,—into ordered line and phrase. It is then as the trees in the ground of some pervenue gardener, trimmed into grotesque architecture and deformity, shorn of their grace and beauty, and mere caricatures of the great forests.

Thackeray will have none of this; he touches the barren rock of dictionary lore and the living words gush forth.

Some of the best examples of his style are found in the introduction of Major Pendennis reading his morning mail, in the perusal of which you get several life histories; in the scene where Colonel Esmond discards the young pretender, and in Colonel Newcome's last hour. In these are shown the marvel and power of a few simple words.

Like music answering music is a younger author's affectionate tribute to the great master.

In his *Letters to Dead Authors,* Lang says of Thackeray's style, using for his text Thackeray's own words, "Forever echoing in the heart and present in the memory:—"

Who has heard these tones, who does

not hear them as he turns over your books that, for so many years have been companions and comforters? We have been young and old, we have been sad and merry with you, we have listened to the midnight chimes with Pen and Warrington, have stood with you beside the death-bed, have mourned at that yet more awful funeral of lost love, and with you have prayed in the inmost chapel sacred to our old and immortal affections, *a leal souvenir!* And whenever you speak for yourself, and speak in earnest, how magical, how rare, how lonely in our literature is the beauty of your sentences! 'I cannot express the charm of them,' so you wrote of George Sand; so we may write of you. They seem to me like the sound of country bells, provoking I don't know what vein of music and meditation, and falling sweetly and sadly on the ear. Surely that style, so fresh, so rich, so full of surprises—that style which stamps as classical your fragments of slang, and perpetually astonishes and delights—would alone give immortality to an author, even had he little to say.

But you with your whole wide world of fops and fools, of good women and brave men, of honest absurdities and cheery adventurers; you who created the Steynes and Newcomes, the Beckys and Blanches, Captain Costigan and F. B. and the Chevalier Strong—all that host of friends imperishable—you must survive with Shakespeare and Cervantes in the memory and affections of men.

When Thackeray grows weary of snobs and their ways, and of the meanness and baseness of life, he has places of refuge, where no evil comes, but only charity and worth and manliness. These are his temples, and some deity of truth is worshipped in each. You can weep and pray with him here, and walk forth with new-opened heart. I liken him to the Ancient Mariner, homeward bound after that voyage of evil sights, who crosses the harbo nr bar, and sees the light-house top, and the kirk and feels the familiar homely flush of life in his own country once more. Straightway his spirit falls prone and he learns the messages he is to take to all, that he prayeth best, who loveth best, all things both great and small. So, when Thackeray comes to the lives of good men and women, he casts off his hardihood and cynicism, and sees only the things that he loves best. If he created Becky Sharpe, and George Osborne and Barnes Newcome, he also gave us the Little Sister, and Amelia Sedley, and dear old Dobbin.

The wickedness and baseness is overmatched by Colonel Newcome, and where in all literature is there so simple, kindly, manly and chivalrous a soul. Almost the first we see of him is in the coffee room when he arises from his seat, trembling with indignation and stalks out with little Clive, because one of the bachanalians commences to sing a ribald song. His life is all one prayer for his boy. When the evil days came and the lash of The Old Campaigner fell upon him, he bowed his shoulders in charity and patience. In the real world it might be hard to find men like him, but unquestionably there are women like her. We last see him in Gray Friars, one of the Poor Brethren accepting with blended pride and humility the dole of charity for a little time until death comes. With Clive, and Ethel, and Madame de Florac, whom he had loved and lost forty years before, clinging to his hands, he heard the evening bell strike as his summons came, and raising his head called "*Adsum,*" the word he answered with when names were called at school. Colonel Newcome alone redeems Thackeray from the charge of thinking too meanly of human kind. His own careless lines best close the page:—

> The play is done; the curtain drops,
> Slow falling to the prompter's bell;
> A moment yet the actor stops,
> And looks around to say farewell.
> It is an irksome work and task;
> And when he's laughed and said his say,
> He shows, as he removes the mask,
> A face that's anything but gay.
>   * * *
> Come wealth or want, come good or ill,
> Let young and old accept their part,
> And bow before the Awful Will,
> And bear it with an honest heart.
> Who misses, or who wins the prize?
> Go, lose or conquer as you can;
> But if you fail, or if you rise,
> Be each, pray God, a gentleman.

DEGENERATION.

In his *Degeneration,* Dr. Nordau comes crashing into literature like the traditionary bull into a china shop. When that rude invasion occurred, according to some accounts, the proprietor of the shop, after the intruder had been led away to the shambles, took an inventory of the ruins. He found great wreckage of silly gingerbreadware, of costly stucco, and antique vases, priceless because they were old; he found broken specimens made famous and notable because some mad fancier had started the fashion of doting on them, and many other sheep-like madmen had chased after their leaders. Some of these fragments were ground into dust and past all patching; but others he noted he could stick together and hide their wounds, or, better still, could parade them maimed and battered in proof of their great antiquity. To maintain my figure properly I choose to believe that this shopkeeper was a collector, a *connoisseur,* a lover of rare old pottery who paid fabulous prices for such as pleased his taste; one who valued many of the gems of his collection, not because they were artistic, but because they were hideous, and other pieces because no one else had them, and still others because some Royal Society had set its approval on them. I shall assume that he had some dingy lies purporting to come from the palaces of Pompeii, or the tombs of Etrusca, that really hailed from the shed of some vile nineteenth century potter. The bull must have knocked some of the grimy deceiving glaze from these gauds and shown them for what they were. Our antiquarian could solace himself with the thought that he could afford to lose some of his wares; could patch others and deceive the public with the fragments, and that after all, his best treasures were on the higher shelves and received no harm. In the case at bar, as the lawyers say, we who keep the literary shop have walked about since Nordau darkened our doors, picking up the ruins and ruefully surveying the broken idols.

We find much dull clay gilded as wedgewood and rare china; we find antiquities that were made yesterday with no more lies to tell; we find that some things can be patched together; and, thankfully, we find that some priceless treasures were placed so high that this raging iconoclast could not harm them. Let us, then, rejoice over our salvage. As for Nordau, he has been led away to the critic's shambles, there to await the lethal strokes of ten thousand daggers.

The vendetta between him and his victims, and victim's victims has become international. It is our happiness to sit around in the pleasant amphitheatre and watch the killing, moved only by the love of truth. Under no circumstances let us turn up our thumbs for the king's mercy. This charge of one man upon an army will be one of the famous braveries in literature. He faced only the leaders at first, "the prime in order and in might," but behind these come the inferior orders, and then the ten thousand thousand disciples of the Degenerates. This rude shock did not even spare the temple of France where the Forty Immortals are safely housed beyond all necessity of struggling for fame. It is vain however to suppose that the common business of establishing cults will be lessened much. We will still continue to give to our newest Genius assurance of fame by naming clubs after him, and disciplining an army to ring his perpetual eulogy. In club circles it will still be thought blasphemous that critics like Nordau should disturb public worship by their rude and fretful speech. We shall spend many a decade hereafter listening to the donkey chorus, and watching the halo, which Dullness always delights to place around Dullness, grow and fade.

I have my own fee-grief however. After reading Nordau, I bethought me of those ancient library favorites—those storehouses of polite letters — The *Poets' Argosy; Treasures of Verse;* and *Sheaves Gleaned From the Great Ocean of Literature.* I fear that I have been harbouring Degenerates behind these wooden walls. I know that the gentle-souled compilers, always thoughtful of the manners and morals of their patrons, have already expurgated much, yet I may have to follow them with the blue pencil. If I must, I shall even tear out a forbidden leaf here and there. If an intimate friend of mine is arrested at my house charged with a heinous crime, shall I go off to gaol and bail him out, and provide for his defense, not caring for my own safety? Or will it be more prudent for me to come out boldly and honestly against him; frankly admit that he may be guilty, and that I have observed suspicious things about him for a long time, as I frequently remarked to my other friend, Smith, as Smith very well knows? Is not this the best way to get away from the ridicule and shame of the matter, especially as I remember trying to make many people believe that my friend in custody was a worthy honest fellow? How can I clear myself of the suspicions arising from my intimacy with the criminal unless I repudiate him utterly? If I have had a sneaking fondness for Swinburne and Maeterlinck, now that Nordau has made his arrest, is it my best policy to attempt a rescue, or, shall I abandon them to their fate; denounce them in an airy off-handed way, and announce that I never approved of them and am glad of their exposure?

Indeed, Nordau says that Degenerates love a Degenerate, and thus I may become classified as a Mattoid, an Egomaniac, or a Graphomaniac, simply because of the company I have kept. These questions as to what faith shall be maintained with old friends are matters of casuistry that the honorable reader will settle for himself.

For my own part, I think that if an author, after having deceived us these many years, now turns out under a new diagnosis to be a Mattoid or other monster, he is not entitled to much consideration, and we owe it to ourselves to look out for ourselves. The dear ladies who have wept sentimentally over Ibsen's multifarious sweet follies; the loveless ones who have 'scaped either matrimony or its happiness, and who find comfort in Tolstoi because he preaches that marriage is not only a failure but a desecration; the ardent devotees of realism who have followed in Zola's furrow as he subsoiled dunghills; the many youths of kindling minds who have been lured by the gorgeous coloring of Swinburne and Rossetti, as the savage is lured by a red blanket and glass beads; those who love the dictionary conglomerates of Maeterlinck, Baudelaire and Nietzsche

—must endure the shock of seeing their deified good masters turned into swine—into Yahoos, whom none shall reverence.

Nordau has the scientist's rage for classifying the unclassifiable. To the layman the task seems as vain as that of the phrenologists who subdivide the human skull into compartments, stocking each with its appropriate tenant. It is urged that Nordau pleads his cause against the Degenerates with too much vehemence; but a juror need not assume that an advocate has a bad case, because he argues it with exaggeration and energy. This new science of Degeneration has begotten names and titles that are appalling to the non-professional reader. How are pupils in the lower forms to know what Masochism, Megalomania, Neo-Catholicism, Graphomania, Anthropomorphism, Zoomorphism, Echolalia and many other titles of strange disease, are? The scholars must supply literature with a new index for its maladies, or else allow us to lump them off under the head of Nervous Prostration or General Debility.

To a native of the upper Mississippi Valley, this baiting and harrying of the Degenerates seems like a visitation of righteous wrath only too long delayed. In places where literature has an established service and a common law of tradition and custom, success seems generally to follow persistent clacking and tickling. You talk up my new poem and I will talk up your new novel; thus pigmy calls to pigmy, and a great deal of noise is made about nothing. If this persistent reciprocal advertising be kept up long enough the Public will soon come to think we are both great men. Would you know how great fame is built up out of nothing, read Nordau's account of the making of Maeterlink.

This pitiable mental cripple vegetated for years wholly unnoticed in his corner of Ghent without the Belgian Symbolists, who outbid even the French, according him the slightest attention; as to the public at large, no one had a suspicion of his existence. Then one fine day in 1890 his writings fell accidentally into the hands of the French novelist, Octave Mirbeau. He read them, and whether he desired to make fun of his contemporaries in grand style, or whether he obeyed some morbid impulsion is not known; it is sufficient to say that he published in *Le Figaro* an article of unheard of extravagance, in which he represented Maeterlinck as the most brilliant, sublime, moving poet which the last three hundred years had produced, and assigned him a place near—nay, above Shakespeare. And then the world witnessed one of the most extraordinary, and most convincing examples of the force of suggestion. The hundred thousand rich and cultivated readers to whom *Figaro* addresses itself immediately took up the views which Mirbeau had imperiously suggested to them. They at once saw Maeterlinck with Mirbeau's eyes. They found in him all the beauties which Mirbeau asserted that he perceived in him. Anderson's fairy tale of the invisible clothes of the emperor repeated itself line for line. They were not there, but the whole court saw them. Some imagined they really saw the absent state robes; the others did not see them, but rubbed their eyes so long that they at least doubted whether they saw them or not; others again could not impose on themselves, but dared not contradict the rest. Thus Maeterlinck became at one stroke, by Mirbeau's favour, a great poet, and a poet of "the future." Mirbeau had also given quotations which would have completely sufficed for a reader who was not hysterical, not given over irresistibly to suggestion, to recognize Maeterlinck for what he is, namely, a mentally debilitated plagiarist; but these very quotations wrung cries of admiration from the *Figaro* public, for Mirbeau had pointed them out as beauties of the highest rank, and every one knows that a decided affirmation is sufficient to compel hypnotic patients to eat raw potatoes as oranges and to believe themselves to be dogs or other quadrupeds.

Nordau gives out this as his text:

Degenerates are not always criminals, prostitutes, anarchists, and pronounced lunatics; they are often authors and artists. These however manifest the same mental characteristics, and, for the most part, the same somatic features as the members of the above anthropological family.

This is his indictment of the great donkey-like public:

> But grievous is the fate of him who has the audacity to characterize æsthetic fashions as forms of mental decay. The author or artist attacked never pardons a man for recognizing in him the lunatic or charlatan; the subjectively garrulous critics are furious when it is pointed out how shallow and incompetent they are, or how cowardly when swimming with the stream; and even the public is angered when forced to see that it has been running after fools, quack dentists, and mountebanks as so many prophets. Some among these degenerates in literature, music and painting have in recent years come into extraordinary prominence, and are revered by numerous admirers as creators of a new art, and heralds of the coming centuries.

He defines Degeneration as "a morbid deviation from an original type." He says:

> The society which surrounds the degenerate always remains strange to him. The Englishman is conquered by an absurdity accompanied by diagrams. Ruskin is one of the most turbid and fallacious minds, and one of the most powerful masters of style of the present century. * * * The Pre-Raphælites who got all their leading principles from Ruskin, went further. They misunderstood his misunderstandings. He had simply said that defectiveness in form can be counterbalanced by devotion and noble feeling in the artist. They, however raised it to the position of a fundamental principle, that in order to express devotion and noble feeling, the artist must be defective in form. * * * If any human activity is individualistic, it is that of the artist. True talent is always personal. In its creations it reproduces itself, its own views and

feelings, and not the articles of faith learned from an æsthetic apostle. If Gœthe had never written a line of verse, he would all the same have remained a man of the world, a man of good principles, a fine art connoiseur, a judicious collector, a keen observer of nature. Lombroso, a very great authority, says of degenerates: "If they are painters, then their predominant attribute will be the color sense; they will be decorative. If they are poets they will be rich in rhyme, brilliant in style, but barren of thought; sometimes they will be decadents."

In this connection it may be said that the curious style of some artists of this generation, notably Monet and his school bears out the above statement. Nordau says of Monet:

Thus originate the violet pictures of Monet and his school which spring from no actual observable aspect of nature, but from the subjective view due to the condition of the nerves. When the entire surface of walls in salons and art exhibitions of the day appears veiled in uniform half-mourning, this predilection for violet is simply an expression of the nervous debility of the painter.

Of our own decadents only Walt. Whitman is taken; perhaps the crop is too small and too immature to merit reaping. This belittlement of those who are spared may be deserved, and yet if Nordau could have read our Tigerish Affection Poetry, our Poetry of Cold Soggy Dreams, or our Small Poetry for Big Magazines, he might have found a trace at least of the deadly virus of degeneration. We do not worship overmuch our home-born degenerates. Some of our attempts at literature are puerile, imitative, and vacuous enough, but it is the silly madness and unreason of childhood rather than the rancid ripeness and putrescent maturity of old-world degeneration. You can readily distinguish between the childish prattle of the kindergarten, and the awful adult babble and clamor of the madhouse.

Our small-and-early literature is so dessicated and unfattened in its life, that it cannot spoil; there is nothing in it for decay to feed upon, and so it dies without the grosser tokens of mortality. The diseases of degeneration must draw nutriment from something having life and power, even though it be of a degraded sort. We have no madmen with burning brains, like Tolstoi, crying in our wilderness; they belong to an older civilization. Our erotic literature has a brief and transitory life; it is infected with a thin, washed-out, enfeebled and innocuous depravity that is impotent to do harm except among school children. Its makers put it up in imitation of Zola, Rossetti and Swinburne, who are as eagles to these midges. The nympho-maniacal young women who write prose and verse for the patient American public deserve to be put in straight-jackets, only they are not worth a *commission de lunatico*. They try to fly as eagles but cannot clear the stye where they seem to live.

Nordau digs up the early remains of the Pre-Raphælites to point his moral. This Brotherhood is referred to as an instance of how men of real talent can indulge in grotesque affectation. Dante Gabriel Rossetti, Holman Hunt and Millais formed the Pre-Raphælite Brotherhood in 1848; Collinson and Stephens, two painters and Woolner, the sculptor, joined later. For a time they marked all their work P. R. B. Nordau says of them:

> In course of time the Pre-Raphælites laid aside many of their early extravagances. Millais and Holman Hunt no

longer practice the affectation of wilfully bad drawing and of childish babbling in imitation of Giotto's language. * * * They did not paint sober visions but emotions. They therefore introduced into their pictures mysterous allusions and obscure symbols which have nothing to do with the visible reality.

Nordau defines Pre-Raphælitism thus:

It is true that the Pre-Raphælites with both brush and pen betray a certain, though by no means exclusive predilection for the Middle Ages; but the mediævalism of their poems and paintings is not historical but mythical, and simply denotes something outside time and space—a time of dreams and a place of dreams, where all unreal figures and actions may be conveniently bestowed. That they decorate their unearthly world with some features which may remotely recall mediævalism; that it is peopled with queens and knights, noble damozels with coronets on their golden hair, and pages with plumed caps—these may be accounted for by the prototypes which, perhaps unconsciously, hover before the eyes of the Pre-Raphælites.

Rossetti finally becomes a man of letters, dominated possibly by his name. William Morris finally joins the Pre-Raphælites, and I am reluctantly compelled to say that he has, on one occasion at least, stolen something besides inspiration from the "mournful Tuscan's haunted rhyme." This practice of conscripting a blessed damozel out of the Middle Ages to do duty in poetry is common with Rossetti and his school. Tennyson—a healthy poet, teaches us that a simple maiden in her flower, is worth a hundred blessed damozels.

In Rossetti's poem "Troy Town," the refrain "O Troy Town," and "O Troy's down," and "Tall Troy's on fire," is tacked on as the alien and unassisting tail-piece to each one of fourteen strophes. Thus:

 Helen knelt at Venus' shrine,
   [O Troy town!]
 Saying, "A little gift is mine,
 A little gift for a heart's desire,
 Hear me speak and make me a sign!
   [O Troy's down,
   Tall Troy's on fire!]"

Nordau says:

He is ever muttering as he goes, monotonously as in a litany, the mysterious invocations to Troy, while he is relating the visit to the temple of Venus at Sparta.

Sollier has the proposition that:

A special characteristic found in literary mattoids, and also, as we have seen, in the insane, is that of repeating some words or phrases hundreds of times in the same page.

His twin brother, Swinburne, is

called upon for his contribution to the poetical crazy quilt.

> We were ten maidens in the green corn,
> Small red leaves in the mill-water;
> Fairer maidens never were born,
> Apples of gold for the King's daughter.
>
> We were ten maidens by a well-head,
> Small white birds in the mill-water;
> Sweeter maidens never were wed,
> Rings of red for the King's daughter.

This mill-water is a monotonous receptacle for almost everything from "small white birds," to "a little wind," and it bears its variegated burdens through many verses to the end; when the final grave is dug for the star daughter, it is still on duty. In the last verse "running rain," is cast in aqueous tautology into the mill-water. This practice of putting a tether on Fancy "skyward flying," and bringing her back with a jerk to the same point after every flight, seems unneccessarily cruel and inharmonious.

The Belgian poet, Maurice Maeterlinck, furnishes rare sport for this hunter of Degenerates. From the *Serres chaudes* of Maeterlinck this sample is given:

O hot-house in the middle of the woods. And your doors ever closed! And all that is under your dome! And under my soul in your analogies! The thoughts of a princess who is hungry; the tedium of a sailor in the desert; a brass-band under the windows of incurables. Go into the warm moist corners! One might say 'tis a woman fainting on harvest-day. In the courtyard of the infirmary are postilions; in the distance an elk-hunter passes by, who now tends the sick. Examine in the moonlight! [O, nothing there is in its place!] One might say, a madwoman before judges, a battle ship in full sail on a canal, night-birds on lilies, a death-knell towards noon [down there under those bells], a halting-place for the sick in the meadows, a smell of ether on a sunny day. My God! My God! when shall we have rain and snow and wind in the hot-house?

To show how easy this is, Nordau writes a parody of it in this fashion:

O Flowers! And we groan so heavily under the very old taxes! An hour-glass, at which the dog barks in May; and the strange envelope of the negro who has not slept. A grandmother who would eat oranges and could not write! Sailors in a ballroom, but blue! blue! On the bridge this crocodile and the policeman with the swollen cheek beckons silently! O two soldiers in the cowhouse, and the razor is notched! But the chief prize they have not drawn. And on the lamp are ink spots!

Nordau despairingly asks: "Why parody Maeterlinck? His style bears no parody, for it has already reached the extreme limits of idiocy. Nor is it quite worthy of a mentally sound man to make fun of a poor devil of an idiot."

Zola and his school do not escape punishment.

M. Zola boasts of his method of work; all his books "emanate from observation." The truth is that he has never "observed;" that he has never, following Gœthe "plunged into the full tide of human life," but has always remained shut up in a world of paper, and has drawn all his subjects out of his own brain, all his "realistic" details from newspapers and books read uncritically. * * * His eyes are never directed towards nature or humanity, but only to his own "Ego." In order that the borrowed detail should remain faithful to reality, it must preserve its right relation to the whole phenomenon, and this is what never happens with M. Zola. To quote only two examples. In *Pot-Bouille,* among the inhabitants of a single house in the Rue de Choiseul, he brings to pass in the space of a few months all the infamous things he has learnt in the course of thirty years, by reports from acquaintances, by cases in courts of law, and various facts from newspapers about apparently honourable bourgeois families; in *La Terre,* all the vices imputed to the French peasantry or rustic people in general, he crams into the character and conduct of a few inhabitants of a small village in Beauce; he may in these cases have supported every detail by cuttings from newspapers, or jottings, but the whole is not the less monstrously and ridiculously untrue. I allowed myself for thirteen years to be led astray by his swagger, and credulously accepted his novels as sociological contributions to the knowledge of French life. The family whose history Zola presents to us in twenty mighty volumes is entirely outside normal daily life, and has no neccessary connection whatever with France and the Second Empire. It might just as well have lived in Patagonia and at the time of the Thirty Years' War.

Nordau says that the history of one family of criminals in France has supplied M. Zola with material for all of his novels. It is comforting to know that the human beasts described in works like *La Terre* are selected cases. Thinking that they were samples of the French people, I have felt like giving voice to Byron's adjuration, slightly paraphrased:

Arise ye Teutons and glut your ire.

A land peopled with Zola's characters would be a carcass that even vultures would disdain.

Nordau says of Friedrich Nietzsche:

As in Ibsen ego-mania has found its poet, so in Nietzsche it has found its philosopher. The deification of filth by the Parnassians with ink, paint and clay; the censing among the diabolists and decadents of licentiousness, disease and corruption; the glorification, by Ibsen of the person who "wills," is "free" and "wholly himself"—of all this Nietzsche supplies the theory, or, something which proclaims itself as such. * * * From the first to the last page of Nietzsche's writings the careful reader seems to hear a madman, with flashing eyes, wild gestures, and foaming mouth, spouting forth deafening bombast; and through it all, now breaking out into frenzied laughter, now sputtering expressions of filthy abuse, and invective, now skipping about in a giddily agile dance, and now bursting upon the auditors with threatening mien and clenched fists. Nietzsche evidently had the habit of throwing on paper with feverish haste all that passed through his head, and when he had collected a heap of these snippings, he sent them to the printer and there was a book. * * * It remains a disgrace to the German intellectual life of the present age, that in Germany a pronounced maniac should have been regarded as a philosopher and have founded a school. In proof of the correctness of the foregoing criticism I take a passage from *Zarathustra*.

"The world is deep and deeper than the day thinks it. Forbear! forbear! I am too pure for thee. Disturb me not! Has not my world become exactly perfect? My flesh is too pure for thy hands. Forbear, thou dull, doltish and obtuse day! Is not the midnight clearer? The purest are to be lords of the earth, the most unknown, the strongest, the souls of midnight who are clearer and deeper than each day. * * * My sorrow, my happiness are deep thou strange day; but yet I am not God, no

Hell of God; deep is their woe. God's woe is deeper, thou strange World! Grasp at God's woe, not at me! What am I? A drunken sweet lyre—a lyre of midnight, a singing frog understood by none, but who must speak before the deaf, O higher men! For ye understand me not! Hence! Hence! O Youth!" etc.

It would make too lengthy a review to do more than refer to what Nordau says of the other French degenerates. Among them, is Verlaine, who was in prison for two years for a hideous crime; with this preparation he comes forth and establishes a school or cult in literature. Stephane Mallarme admired as a great poet in certain circles in France, but who affected silence, with the pretension that it was indelicate and vulgar to expose his naked soul in print. From the top of the pedestal where his worshippers placed him he stimulates their adoration by speechless posturing, leaving them to read without the aid of the ink-well the great thoughts which they credulously attribute to him. With these comes Moreas, another leader of the Symbolists. Leaving France, we fly at higher game in Tolstoi. Nordau says of him:

> He has become in the last few years one of the best known, and apparently, also, one of the most widely read authors in the world. Every one of his words awakens an echo among all the civilized nations on the globe. His strong influence over his contemporaries is unmistakable. The universal success of Tolstoi's writings is undoubtedly due in part to his high literary gifts. * * * Tolstoi would have remained unnoticed like any Knudson of the seventeenth century, if his extravagances as a degenerate mystic had not found his contemporaries prepared for their reception. The wide-spread hysteria from exhaustion

was the requisite soil in which alone Tolstoi could flourish. In England it was Tolstoi's sexual morality that excited the greatest interest, for in that country economic reasons condemn a formidable number of girls, particularly of the educated classes, to forego marriage; and from a theory which honored chastity as the highest dignity and noblest human destiny, and branded marriage with gloomy wrath as abominable depravity, these poor creatures would naturally derive rich consolation for their lonely, empty lives and their cruel exclusion from the possibility of fulfilling their natural calling. The *Kreutzer Sonata* has, therefore, become the book of devotion of all the spinsters of England. * * * Lombroso instances a certain Knudson, a madman, who lived in Schleswig about 1680, and asserted that there was neither a God nor a hell; that priests and judges were useless and pernicious, and marriage an immorality; that men ceased to exist after death; that every one must be guided by his own inward insight, etc. Here we have the principal features of Tolstoi's cosmology and moral philosophy. Kundson has, however, so little pointed out leading the way to those coming after, that he still only exists as an instructive case of mental abberation in books on diseases of the mind.

Nordau's work would be incomplete without an exposition of Ibsenism. He says of Ibsen:

> That Henrik Ibsen is a poet of great verve and power is not for a moment to be denied. He is extraordinarily emotive, and has the gift of depicting in an exceptionally life-like and impressive manner that which has excited his feelings. * * * Similarly it must be acknowledged that Ibsen has created some characters possessing a truth to

life and a completeness such as are not to be met with in any poet since Shakespeare. Gina, in *The Wild Duck*, is one of the most profound creations of world-literature—almost as great as Sancho Panza, who inspired it. Ibsen has had the daring to create a female Sancho, and in his temerity has come very near to Cervantes, whom no one has equaled. If Gina is not quite so overpowering as Sancho, it is because there is wanting in her his contrast to Don Quixote.

Through many pages of Nordau, Ibsen is dissected and examined. Ibsen's childish ignorance of the simplest facts taught by modern science; his silly expositions and illustrations of the effect of heredity; his habit of mounting little hobbyhorses that have already been ridden to death by the authors of the Sunday-school literature of a generation back; the artless discussions carried on by his characters, of delicate and complex social problems, are all given by Nordau as signs of Degeneration.

I should rather say that these things were proofs that Ibsen was a mere dreamer, lacking accuracy; one who was but a shallow student of facts and social problems, and who has had but slight training as a man of the world and of affairs. He has but a dry and tedious closet-wisdom, yet it is sugar-coated at times with his rare poetic and dramatic gifts. It would be a far deduction to say that these faults denoted Degeneration. They rather strongly prove the vaguely nebulous condition of thought, incident to one in his non-age. His ideas of sacrifice, of expiation for sin; his doctrine that men and women must live out their lives, which he explains to mean that they should follow their own sensual or selfish impulses no matter at what cost or shame to others; his open abandonment of all these theories and the advocacy of their opposites from time to time as fits his mood, are certainly marks of mental and moral perversion. If he have a sound lesson on the necessity of right living, to-day, he is sure to contradict it on some other day with guileless and shameless inconsistency. His career is like that of the Libyan who wished to become a god. With this purpose he caged a large number of parrots and taught them to say "Apsethus, the Libyan is a god." Then he set them loose and they spread all over Lybia, and repeated in every wood what he had taught them. The Libyans not knowing of his trick were astounded and finally came to regard him as a god. Nordau uses this story as illustrative of Ibsen, and adds:

In imitation of the ingenious

Apsethus, Ibsen has taught a few "comprehensives," Brandes, Eberhards, Jægers, etc.—the words "Ibsen is a modern," "Ibsen is a poet of the future," and the parrots have spread over all the lands and are chattering with deafening din in books and papers, "Ibsen is great!" "Ibsen is a modern spirit!" and imbeciles among the public murmur the cry after them, because they hear it frequently repeated, and because on such as they, every word uttered with emphasis and assurance makes an impression.

No enthronement however high is safe from Nordau; he invades temples that a humbler critic may not enter even on tiptoe. He confronts the mighty Wagner in his pride of place and shows the plague-spots in his character. I copy only a fragment from this arraignment:—

The shamless sensuality which prevails in his dramatic poems has impressed all his critics. Hanslick speaks of the "bestial sensuality" in Rheingold, and says of Siegfried: "The feverish accents so much beloved by Wagner, of an insatiable sensuality, blazing to the uttermost limits—this ardent moaning, sighing, crying, sinking to the ground, move us with repugnance. The text of these love-scenes becomes sometimes in its exuberance, sheer nonsense." Compare in the first act of the Walkure, in the scene between Siegmund and Sieglinde, the following stage direction: "Hotly interrupting;" "embraces her with fiery passion;" "in gentle ecstacy;" "she hangs enraptured upon his neck;" "close to his eyes;" "beside himself;" "in the highest intoxication," etc. At the conclusion, it is said "the curtain falls quickly," and frivolous critics have not failed to perpetrate the cheap witticism, "very necessary, too." The amorous whinings, whimperings and ravings of Tristan and Isolde, the entire second act of Parsifal, in the scene between the hero and the flower-girls, and then between him and Kundry in Klingsor's magic garden, are worthy to rank with the above passages. It certainly redounds to the high honour of German public morality, that Wagner's operas could have been publicly performed without arousing the greatest scandal. How unperverted must wives and maidens be when they are in a state of mind to witness these pieces without blushing crimson and sinking into the earth for shame! How innocent must even husbands and fathers be who allow their womankind to go to these representations of "lupanar" incidents! Evidently the German audiences entertain no misgivings concerning the actions and attitudes of Wagnerian personages; they seem to have no suspicion of the emotions by which they are excited, and what intention their words, gestures and acts denote; and this explains the peaceful artlessness with which these audiences follow theatrical scenes during which, among a less childlike public, no one would dare to lift his eyes to his neighbour or endure his glance.

This new science of Degeneration has enriched our vocabulary with odd grotesque forms of speech, but lately sprung up in the madhouses, dissecting rooms and hospitals; the doctors have been plagiarized and their livery stolen for the service of literature. So dressed forth, Nordau's clinic becomes too physiological for the *Critics' Corner* in a ladies' magazine, even if in that locality we could endure so strong an antidote to the gentle adjacent gush. The critics who hover as vultures alike over the mountain peaks of genius and the dead plains of mediocrity will have rare feasting on what Nordau has left; he has certainly run the game to earth for them.

The art of criticism has always owed much to the earlier classics. They furnished it inspiration, names, titles, figures, and illustrations. One hundred and fifty years ago no critical discourse would have been thought worthy a place in letters if it did not contain industrious gleanings from mythology; critics hunted from Rome back to Troy for whips with which to scourge offenders against their laws. Homer was the most constant source of supply; now his verses, (if I may use a bit of jesting vernacular,) have become back-numbers. I detest Smith's absurd book of essays; if I reviewed it in the style of the last century, I would call him a modern Theresites, or compare him to some other equally unvalued ancient; or I would suggest that he had found some bog-hole and drank from it under the mistake that it was the

Pierian Spring. All this is old style, and was very well in its day.

With the aid of this new science, I call Smith, a Literary Mattoid, an Egomaniac, a Phraseomaniac, or some other of the hospital-coined titles and epithets. It will be so much more puzzling and painful for Smith, when he shall find that his essays are not damned by the dictionary, and that in order to know what it is that I have called him, he must consult his medical man. A more serious thought that may well give us pause, is, what effect do these new discoveries have on the law of libel and slander? Is the term Mattoid, when applied to an author, actionable? What should be the rule of damages for an author who has been called on Egomaniac? Is the term Nymphomaniac calculated to excite an assault and breach of the peace, and therefore indictible? Some of these questions will unhappily find an answer in court, and I will not prejudice the final judgment by any hasty opinion.

This excursion into Darkest Literature, has all the fascinations attending new discoveries in lands of strange beasts and birds and men,—

" * * * whatever title please thine ear
Whether thou choose Cerventes serious air
Or laugh and shake in Rabelais' easy chair."

Quoting Pope is a reminder that Degeneration has not yet been called the nineteenth century Dunciad—an omission which is, I fancy, entitled to some comendation. Yet prompted now, so strong is the habit of fashioning the divine parallel, we recur to that earlier Dunciad in search of all marks of likeness or difference. Pope, probably a degenerate himself, hunted his enemies like a ferret out of the ratholes of Grub Street; yet he distils his poison in courtly numbers, and fair-sounding verse. He runs the Dunciad in heroic mould, and puts Theresites mockingly into the shining armour of Achilles. He compels the mogrel mob in his Kingdom of Dullness to walk in god-like struts before he jeeringly dispatches them to the shades. A dunce is more of a dunce dressed in the rhetorical frippery of old gods and kings, just as the ass in the fable who puts on the lion's hide, thereby becomes more of an ass. Pope's heroic rhyme is like a parade of gloriously equipped warriors sent out apparently to honourable battle, only finally to be employed as catchpoles for curbstone criminals. The rhyming garniture of the Dunciad with its myriad harmonies has some obscurities that somewhat dim the wit after so long a time. There is a species of wit indigenous to time and place; it will not bear transplanting, and withers a little in a strange environment. After nearly two centuries have passed, we lose the point of much of this venom-dripping rhyme; the near-by audience laughed it to the echo. We cannot bring back that fretting, fuming Bohemia where Pope was king. One must have seen the fribbling rout of vulgar pretenders whom Pope left howling, in order to take full pleasure in their correction. We should go back to Will's, and hear the daily gossip that ranged from the street to the chambers of great noblemen, to make us apt in the study of this devilish delicate wit. Who can interpret it now, or pluck the full meaning of these fleshless jests from their graveyard? No more can we tell all that Rabelais and Swift meant by their stupendous satires.

As Hamlet in sad derision picked up the skull of poor Yorick, so do we take up the Dunciad. It was a thing of infinite jest once; but now, where be its gibes? its gambols? its flashes of merriment that were wont to set the table on a roar? All are gone and we are sitting gazing at a stage-full of mere skeletons of jests whose appearance once shook the galleries.

Nordau on the other hand has constructed for us a scientific treatise—a text book; a cold phlegmatic analysis that will be understood in distant times, and without the aid of local history. He does not adorn his labour with the coloring of divine fancy as the ancients decked victims for the sacrifice. He does not waste strength on glowing verse and cunningly turned phrases; he has no place for these in his *materia medica*. He assumes a sterner task, and stands, knife in hand, coolly dissecting and expounding—the genius of the lecture-room.

JOHN SMITH.

I find from my daily that the Smith family is to hold a reunion near Altoona on August 19. It is needless to say that this reunion will be largely attended. Those in charge of the affair have issued a large number of invitations to members of the family in all parts of the world. On these invitations appears a sort of a family tree, being a statement of the fecundity and antiquity of the Smiths. It states that the name antedates the building of King Solomon's Temple by forty years, and the Christian era by 1855 years. There will doubtless be presented at this reunion, a book of Chronicles of the Smith Family, compiled by some enthusiastic Smith, with veracious accounts of how knightly de Smiths won honour in many great battles from Leuctra to Agincourt. Letters are to be read at this gathering from famous absent Smiths and addresses made by famous attendant Smiths. "Invitations," so my account runs, "have been sent to the Italian Smithis, the Spanish Smithos, the German Schmidts, the French Smeets, the Russian Smithtowskis, the Greek Smikons, and the Turkish Seefs." I cannot find from this legend whether the invitations were sent to the Smythes, and the Smithes, but these aristocrats may have been omitted from this felicitation, by the plain Smiths, who constitute the majority of the clan. Caste is a dreadful thing, but it seems to have crept like an alphabetical serpent into the Smith family in the form of the interpolated *y* or *e*. To those afflicted with this aristocratic addition, I would say that the greatest member of the Smith family was plain Smith, with his name-plainness still further accentuated by the Christian name of John. Not to wear this matter out;—I mean Captain John Smith, who fought robbers in England and France, and pirates on the Mediterranean, who did great deeds against the Turk, cutting off the heads of three Turkish champions before the walls of Regall; who bore Turkish and Indian captivity with undaunted soul, and found in the thick darkness of that captivity a glowing romance of love; who was saved from death by an Indian girl, and who performed so many prodigies of valour as to pale "what resounds in fable or romance of Uther's son begirt with British and Armoric knights." The Knights of the Table Round with all their fabled prowess taken for true, could not show his fellow. He was the peer of them all, the courtliest, the bravest and the greatest of soul of all the brave gentlemen adventurers that England sent into far countries three hundred years ago. All that was said of the peerless Launcelot could be said of our captain:

Thou were head of all Christian knights; and thou were the courtiest knight that ever bare shield; and thou were the truest friend to thy lover that ever bestrode horse; and thou were the truest lover of a sinful man that ever loved woman; and thou were the kindest man that ever strake with sword; and thou were the goodliest person ever came among press of knights; and thou were the meekest man and the gentlest that ever ate in hall among ladies; and thou were the sternest knight to thy mortal foe that ever put spear in rest.

Hero worship may run an unchecked

course with this great-hearted man, for all about him seems to have been fine and worthy. The chance which selects parents for great men gave him those by the name of Smith as if in derision of the paltry birthright of a name. His parents followed this commonplace, in an age when there were plenty of Mortimers and Percys by giving their eaglet the name of John. It was later Smiths who have been tempted from the pathway of plain and unromatic orthœpy to insert the extra vowel. But our Smith could afford to wear his name plain, as a prince can afford to wear plain clothes.

He was born of good family in Willoughy, Lincolnshire, in 1579. Lord Bacon, then a young man of nineteen, was studying law at one of the Inns of Court. One Sir Thomas Coke was in a large practice before the courts at Westminster; Queen Elizabeth was in the midst of her long and glorious reign; and there was much fighting and blood-letting going on all over the globe. Spain was wasting the Netherlands with fire and sword. The Turks were in continual war with the nations of southern and western Europe. Eight years before Smith's birth the great battle of Lepanto was fought between the Turks and the Spanish, Italians, and Venetians under Duke John of Austria. Cervantes served as a common soldier in this battle under the banner of Spain. It shattered the sea-power of the Turks, but on land they continued to terrorize Europe until John Sobeski turned them back before the walls of Vienna one hundred years later. It was in this same year of 1579 that Sir Walter Raleigh and his half-brother, Sir Humphrey, sailed for America on a voyage of discovery under a patent from the queen, giving them the right "to discover and take possession of such remote, heathen, and barbarous lands as were not actually possessed by any Christians, or inhabited by any Christian people." Rome was at open war with England, and Pope Gregory issued his famous bull against the heretic nation. As for Spain and France, war was chronic between them and England. Spain was then a mighty power. She held sway over a portion of Italy and over the Low Countries. Her generals were able and ruthless. She had plundered the New World of countless treasure in gold and silver, and scores of her galleons were engaged in bringing the spoil home. A papal decree gave the New World to Spain, but Englishmen were hurrying to dispute this claim. It was in 1580 that Drake dropped anchor in Plymouth harbour, having completed the circuit of the globe, bringing back with him half a million of Spanish treasure. Queen Elizabeth honoured the great freebooter with knighthood, and wore some of the jewels he had taken from the Spaniard in her crown. This was one of the causes that led Phillip to send the great Armada against England, a few years later. By the queen's command Drake again despoiled the Spanish cities in the New World. In these stirring times young Smith grew up. The tales of Drake's adventures, and of the struggle in the Netherlands, and of the Armada with its wreck of ships strewn along the Scottish coast, must have inflamed his youthful imagination, for at the age of thirteen, he sold his books and satchel and started to run away to sea. His father's death, however, kept him at home for a time, and his guardians, solid business men, would have none of youthful folly and so apprenticed him to a merchant at Lynn. This merchant tyrannically refused to allow his apprentice to go to sea, and so Smith went without leave to France with a son of Lord Willoughby. From there he went to the Netherlands where there was good fighting and engaged with the Spaniards for three or four years, under an Englishman, one Captain Druxbury, who was in the service of Prince Maurice. He finally sailed for Scotland, was shipwrecked on the voyage, but escaped without harm, and came again to Willoughby, but not to engage in the arts of peace. He turned hermit. To use his narrative:

> Where, within a short time, being glutted with too much company, wherein he took small delight; he retired himselfe into a little woodie pasture, a good way from any towne, environed with many hundred Acres of other woods. Here by a faire brook he built a Pavillion of boughes, where only in his cloaths he lay. His studie was Machiavill's Art of

Warre, and Marcus Aurelius; his food was thought to be more of venison than anything else; what he wanted his man brought him. The countrey wondering at such an Hermite * * * Long these pleasures could not content him, but he returned againe to the Low-Countreyes.

This effort not to commit himself directly to the venison, seems to have been out of delicate respect for the game laws which were then hanging matter. Hence the expression "His food was thought to be more of venison,—" as if he was simply giving the neighbourhood rumour, rather than admitting a fact against himself. In going into the Low Countries, his plan was to hunt up the Turks and fight with them as soon as possible. He thought himself fitted for this warfare for he says of his acquirements:

Thus when France and the Netherlands had taught him to ride a Horse and use his Armes, with such rudiments of warre as his tender yeeres in those martial Schooles could attaine unto; he was desirous to see more of the world, and trie his fortune against the Turkes; both lamenting and repenting to have seen so many Christians slaughter one another.

Various side adventures caused him to deviate from his purpose to immediately fight the Turks. He was nineteen years of age when he arrived in France. On the voyage over, four robbers stole his baggage, and he had to sell his cloak to pay his passage. He landed in Picardy and went in pursuit of the robbers. He was in great poverty, and, as he says:

But wandring from Port to Port to finde some man-of-war, spent that he had; and in a Forest, neere dead with griefe and cold, a rich Farmer found him by a faire Fountaine under a tree. This kind Pesant releeved him againe to his content, to follow his intent.

Soon after he found Cursell, one of his robbers, and, to follow his narrative:

His piercing injuries had so small patience, as without any word they both drew, and in a short time Cursell fell to the ground, when, from an ruinated Tower, the inhabitants seeing them were satisfied, when they heard Cursell confesse what had formerly passed.

He next came to the chateaux of a noble earl in Brittainy, whom he had known in England, and was hospitably treated there, and from there he journeyed over France for a time, surveying fortresses and other notable objects. At Marseilles he took a ship for Rome. His voyage was not a happy one and he describes the ship's company thus:

Here the inhuman Provincialls, with a rabble of Pilgrims of divers Nations going to Rome, hourely cursing him, not only for a Hugenoit, but his Nation they swore were all Pyrats, and so vildly railed on his dread Soveraigne Queene Elizabeth, and that they never should have faire weather so long as hee was aboard them; their disputations grew to that passion, that they threw him overboard; yet God brought him to that little Isle, where was no inhabitants, but a few kine and goats.

He did not allow this indignity however, without breaking a good many heads. The next day a French ship, the Britaine bound for Alexandria took him off, and he grew into great favour with the captain. This was always his way; he always landed on his feet. Fortune was continually reducing him to a last gasp and then suddenly restoring him to comfort and safety. Soon after, the Britaine fell in with a large Venetian ship with a rich cargo. There did not seem to be any particular occasion for a battle, but of course there had to be one, and it arose over a little discourtesy on the part of the Venetian. The Britaine hailed her and she replied with a shot that killed a sailor on the Britaine. A terrific battle ensued, out of which the Britaine came off victor. The Venetian ship had lost twenty men and was ready to sink, and so part of the cargo was transferred to the Britaine. Smith was no deadhead in this fight, but bore his part, and when it was over, he received for his share of the spoil "five hundred chicqueenes, and a little box God sent him worth neere as much more." In those days piety of the approved sort always had Divine assistance. The spoil must have been great, for Smith says:

 The Silkes, Velvets, Cloth of gold and Tissue, Pyasters, Chicqueenes and Sultanies, which is gold and silver, they unloaded in four and twentie houres, was wonderfull; whereof having sufficient, and tired with toile, they cast her off with her company, with as much good merchandise as would have fraughted another Britaine, that was but two hundred Tunnes, she foure or five hundred.

He landed at Piedmont and thence traveled through Italy, into Dalmatia and Albania. At Rome he said it was "his chance to cee Pope Clement the eight, with many Cardinalls, Creepe up the holy Stayres, which they say are those our Saviour Christ went up to Pontius Pilate." He was still eager to fight the Turks, and finally came to the court of Archduke Ferdinand of Austria, "where he met an English man and an Irish Jesuite; who acquainted him with many brave Gentlemen of a good qualitie." Soon after he joined the army, the Turks beseiged Olympcha.

Smith suggested to Baron Kissell, one of his superior officers, that he could devise a system of telegraphic fires and communicate with the beseiged. To quote from Smith's narrative:

> Kisell inflamed with this strange invention; Smith made it so plain, that forthwith hee gave him guides, who in the darke night brought him to a mountaine, where he showed three torches equidistant from each other which plainly appearing to the Towne; the Governour presently apprehended, and answered againe with three other fires in like manner; each knowing the others being and intent; Smith, thought distant seven miles, signified to him these words; On Thursday at night I will charge on the East, at the Alarum, salley you. Ebersbaught, commander of the city, answered that he would, and thus it was done.

Smith has preserved for us the

alphabet and signals that he used. By means of this plan the Duke's army and the beseiged acted in concert and the Turks were defeated with great slaughter and compelled to raise the seige. In this same battle Smith contrived a plan to deceive the Turks as to the point of attack, by arranging on a line two or three thousand pieces of match, which were fired all at once, that it might appear that there was the Duke's force with its matchlocks. Barely twenty-one years of age, after this battle, Smith was given command of a company of two hundred and fifty men. At the seige of Stowlle-Wesenburg in 1601, Smith's inventive genius was again called into play. He prepared some bombs by filling earthern pots with various explosive and inflammable substances, together with musket balls. These were thrown among the Turks from slings. He describes the effect:

At midnight upon the Alarum, it was a fearful sight to see the short flaming course of their flight in the aire; but presently after their fall, the lamentable noise of the miserable slaughtered Turks was most wonderfull to heare.

Smith, with most excellent naivete, entitles these devices thus:— "An excellent stratagem by Smith;" "Another, not much worse." In this siege the Christians took the town by storm, "with such merciless execution, as was most pittiful to behold." At the battle of Girke, soon after, the Turks were again defeated, but Smith lost half his regiment. Appealing to his narrative again:

Captain Smith had his horse slaine under him, and himselfe sore wounded; but he was not long unmounted *for there was choice enough of horses that wanted masters.*

Soon after the Christian army

beseiged Regall in the Transylvania, a place supposed to be almost impregnable. Now Smith gives us one of the most dramatic incidents of war:

* * * they spent neere a month in entrenching themselves and raising their mounts to plant their batteries. Which slow proceedings the Turkes often derided, that the Ordnance were at pawne, and how they grew fat for want of exercise; and fearing lest they should depart ere they could assault their citie, sent this Challenge to any Captaine in the Armie. That to delight the ladies, who did long to see some court-like pastime, the Lord Turbashaw did defie any Captaine, that had command of a Company, who durst combat with him for his head. The matter being discussed, it was accepted; but so many questions grew for the undertaking, it was decided by lots; which fell upon Captaine Smith, before spoken of.

With this luck to favour him, Smith rode before the armies and met My Lord Turbashaw in mortal combat, unhorsed him and cut off his head. "The head hee presented to the Lord Moses, the Generall, who kindly accepted it; and with joy to the whole armie he was generally welcomed." He tells us also that the "Rampiers were all beset with faire Dames, and men in Armes." The *ennui* of the Turks not being sufficiently dissipated, they sent another challenge to Smith to meet one Grualgo, a friend of Turbashaw. The dauntless Smith took his head, and sent his body and rich apparel back to his friends. No more challenges coming from the Turkish camp, Smith took the initiative. " * * * to delude time, Smith with so many uncontradictable perswading reasons, obtained leave that the Ladies might know he was not so much enamoured of their servants' heads, but if any Turke of their ranke would come to the place of combate to redeeme them, should have his also upon like conditions, if he could winne it." Bonny Mulgro, a Turkish Lord, accepted this challenge and the combatants met with great fury before the armies. The first advantage was with the Turk, and Smith lost his battle axe.

"The Turk prosecuted his advatage to the uttermost of his power; yet the other, what by the readiness of his horse, and his judgment and dexterity in such a businesse, beyond all mens' expectation, by God's assistance, not only avoided the Turke's violence, but having drawne his Faulchion, pierced the Turke so under the Culets thorow backe and body, that although he alighted from his horse, he stood not long ere hee lost his head, as the rest had done."

Smith goes on to say:

This good success gave such great encouragement to the whole Armie, that with a guard of six thousand, three spare horses before each, a Turke's head upon a Lance, he was conducted to the Generall's Pavillion with his Presents. Moyses received both him and them with as much respect as the occasion deserved, embracing him in his armes, gave him a faire Horse richly furnished, a Semitere and belt worth three hundred ducats; and Meldritch made him Sergeant of his regiment.

These valourous performances of Smith before the walls of Regall are worthy to be told of Saladin or Richard the Lion-hearted, or of an earlier chivalry. I cannot find that there were any Christian ladies watching these combats, but there must have been, for Smith never lacked all the accessories of valour. With the Turkish ladies watching from the "Rampieres," it would have been cruel in Fortune, ever so kindly to Smith, not to have supplied the scene with tearful Christian ladies to welcome him back from the fearful field, to bind his bruises and refresh him with words of praise, and to rejoice over the downfall of the cruel Turk, the enemy of all women, Turkish or Christian. After a desperate struggle the Christian army took Regall by storm and all Turks that could bear arms were put to death. To kill Turks in those days was considered a work of great merit. The superfluous youth of every European country, thronged to do battle with the hated Turk. England sent her share of these, and Smith gives the roster of the English dead in the next great battle that was fought with the Turks—Rotenton—in which the Christian army was cut to pieces. We take up Smith's narrative:

And thus in this bloudy field, neere

30,000 lay; some headlesse, armlesse, and leglesse, all cut and mangled; where breathing their last, they gaue this knowledge to the world that for the liues of so few, the Crym-Tartar neuer paid dearer. Give mee leave to remember the names of our owne Country-men with him in those exploits, that as resolutely as the best in the defence of Christ and his Gospell ended their dayes, as Baskerfield, Hardwick, Thomas Milmer, Robert Mullineaux, Thomas Bishop, Francis Compton, George Davison, Nicholas Williams, and one John, a Scot, did what men could doe, and when they could doe no more, left there their bodies in testimonie of their mindes; only ensign Carleton, and Sergeant Robinson escaped. But Smith, among the slaughtered dead bodies, and many a gasping soule with toile and wounds, lay groaning among the rest, till being found by the Pillagers, hee was able to live; and perceiving by his armor and habit his ransome might be better to them than his death, they led him prisoner with many others.

Smith was sold into slavery at Axapolis, and purchased by one Bashaw Bogall, who sent him as a present to his mistress in Constantinople, assuring her that the slave was a great Bohemian Lord whom he had overcome. "This Noble gentlewoman," as Smith calls her, took a more than friendly interest in her sale. She could talk Italian and feigned herself sick that she might make occasion to talk with him. She was bound to know whether Bogall really took him prisoner, or whether this was a boast. Smith told her that he was an "English-man, onely by his adventures made a Captaine in those Countreyes." He won her like another Othello, for he could say:

She loved me for the dangers I had pass'd,

And I loved her that she did pity them.

He says:—

She tooke muche compassion on him; but having no use for him, lest her mother should sell him, she sent him to her brother, the Tymor Bashaw of Nalbritz in the Countrey of Cambia, a province of Tartaria. * * * To her unkinde brother, this kinde Ladie writ so much for his good usage, that he halfe suspected as much as she intended; for shee told him, he should there but sojourne to learne the language, and what it was to be a Turk, till time made her Master of her selfe.

The brother was very wroth that his sister should entertain an affection for a Christian dog, and so he treated Smith with great cruelty, put him in irons and made him a slave of other slaves. He was "no more regarded than a beast." Smith says of this period:

All the hope he ever had to be

delivered from this thraldome was only the love of Tragbigzanda, who surely was ignorant of his bad usage.

This is his last reference to his Turkish mistress. Smith did not forget her, however, for fourteen years later when he was surveying the coast of New England, he named what is now Cape Ann, Cape Tragbigzanda, after her. Prince Charles, with no respect for sentiment, changed this name to Cape Ann. Otherwise this sand dune would have been to this day a geographical monument to the gallant Captain's earliest romance. How this bit of Turkish color on the map would have lighted up the horn-books. Smith finally killed his master, the Bashaw, with a threshing bat and made his way into the wilderness. After days of wandering and much suffering, he came to a Russian outpost on the river Don, and thence found his way into Transylvania, where he was received as one arisen from the dead, with great rejoicing. He says "he was glutted with content, and neere drowned with joy." He came to the camp of his commander, Duke Sigismund. The Duke gave him a sum equal to five hundred pounds sterling of English money and a patent of arms. This patent is dated December 9th, 1603, and Smith had it recorded in the Herald's Office at London, August 19th, 1625. I give some of its quaint recitals:

* * * we have given leave and license to John Smith, an English Gentleman, Captain of 250 Soldiers, etc. * * * Wherefore out of our love and favour according to the law of Armes, We have ordained and given him in his shield of Armes, the figure and description of three Turks heads, which with his sword, before the towne of Regall, he did overcome, kill, and cut off in the Province

of Transilvania. But fortune, as she is very variable, so it chanced and happened to him in the Province of Wallachia in the yeare of our Lord 1602, the 18th day of November, when he with many others, as well Noble men, as also divers other Souldiers, were taken prisoners by the Lord Bashaw of Cambia, a Country of Tartaria; whose cruelty brought him such good fortune, by the helpe and power of Almighty God, that hee delivered himselfe, and returned againe to his company and fellow souldiers; of whom We doe discharge him, and this be hath in witnesse thereof, being much more worthy of a better reward; and now intends to return to his owne sweet Country.

Smith says of this:—

With great honour hee gave him three Turkes heads in a Shield for his Armes, by Patent, under his hand and Seale, with an Oath ever to weare them in his V

Colours, his Picture, [i. e., Sigismund's portrait] ib. Gould and three hundred Ducats, yearely for a pension.

What would not some of our tuft hunters, who buy coats of arms and disport them in gaudy and meretricious state, give for the right to bear such a title of nobility as this? With all our spleen against titles, the most ardent republican might yield to temptation, if he could claim such a token of noble rank as this. But for one fact, I would not answer for the virtue of the most ambitious of the republican Smiths; no Smith can claim to be the lineal descendant of this coat of arms, for he who earned it with his valour, died a bachelor. Unless, indeed, he should have the undiscriminating pride of race of a certain worthy lady I once knew, who claimed to be a lineal descendant of Queen Elizabeth.

After parting with Duke Sigismund,

Smith traveled through Germany, France and Spain, and finally determined to go and fight in the civil wars in Morocco. He sailed in a French ship for Africa, but changed his purpose, and brave as he was does not hesitate to record that this was—

> By reason of the uncertaintie, and the perfidious, treacherous, bloudy murthers rather than warre, among those perfidious, barbarous Moores.

He did not lack occasion for his courage, however, for presently the French ship fell in with two Spanish men-of-war, and they had a brave sea fight lasting for two days. The Frenchman finally beat off the Spaniards with the loss of an hundred men. This ends Smith's adventures on the continent. He returned to England in 1604.

Fitting out expeditions for the New World had by this time become a gentleman's adventure, and many men of high degree joined in these expeditions. After the voyages of the Cabots under English authority in 1598, England remained inactive in the New World for about one hundred years. The Cabots had sailed from Labrador to Florida, touching here and there along the coast. Yet upon this slender scintilla of discovery England before a hundred years had passed, claimed sovereignty over the continent from sea to sea. She was always equal to such claims. She calmly took seisin of a continent by the simple act of going ashore for wood, water or the casual circumstances of a trade of glass beads with some Indians. The other European nations spent a century or two trying to get used to this British habit of claiming the most of the earth. The impact of the beef-eaters was too much for them. By right of the discovery of

Cabot, who was the first white man to see the continent of North America, England wrested the Hudson from the Dutch and absorbed the Swedish settlements on the Delaware, and fought with France over territory for about a hundred years, and finally compelled her ancient enemy to yield up every foot of land east of the Mississippi. In like manner she at a later date reached for India, seized Australia and New Zealand, and innumerable islands, and will soon have Africa in her grasp. It is comforting to put the responsibility for this outreaching on Destiny.

When she parted company with her children on this side of the Atlantic, she bequeathed to them a generous portion of Destiny. Americans took Texas from the weaker Mexicans, and then California. Spain yielded up Florida because she must have known we were bound to have it anyway. Napoleon probably had the same fear when he sold us Louisiana, for our western pioneers, for years before he sold it had been threatening to break through the French barrier at the mouth of the Mississippi. We had an attack of Destiny lately and annexed Haiwai. Next comes Porto Rico, and the Philippines, and by and by, Cuba. Between spells we have dispossessed the Indians of nearly all the lands they once held. In view of our record it seems a huge jest to see our pharisees and devotees of the gospel of cant, grow tender-hearted over England's greed for territory. How we do pity the poor Boer, and the enslaved Hindoo. When a few missionaries' sons stole Haiwai from the simple natives, we blandly received this acquisition and thanked God we are not as Englishmen are. At a time when we owned millions of slaves we were holding mass meetings to denounce the oppression of Ireland.

Thus securely enthroned upon her virtuous pedestal Columbia has made great discoveries of motes in her neighbours' eyes. Occasionally she will vacate her coign of vantage long enough to grab a few principalities that may happen to be lying around loose. But her eyes are always rolled heavenward in holy contemplation of the beatitudes of "equal rights," and of "government by the consent of the governed." All would be well and we should at least escape the charge of hypocrisy, if we would drop Cant, and boldly avow that England or America, or any other civilized nation has the right to seize and hold and police the lands of blood and barbarism, and make them a safe abiding place for native and stranger alike.

After having exhausted the pleasures of European warfare, Smith came to England, and threw himself with ardour into the colonization of the New World. He sailed with an expedition for the American continent in 1606. On the way out he was accused of conspiracy and imprisoned, but on reaching America, he established his innocence and was liberated and admitted to The Council. The lives of all the men who plotted against him were afterwards at his mercy, but he spared them. Once again his life was attempted by secret plotters in his own force, but he escaped, although at this time he was badly injured by a gunpowder explosion.

Every schoolboy knows his adventures in Virginia. He was great-hearted, devoted, and untiring, the life and soul of the infant colonies, and proved that he was born for counsel as well as for war. He had the craft of Ulysses in his dealings with the Indians, and though he was severe towards their treacheries, he was humane. His treaties with them, his many hairbreadth escapes, his battles with them, his capture and rescue from death by the Indian maiden, Pocahontas, are familiar tales. They cannot be recounted within the bounds of this sketch. Posterity has made him the central figure of one heroic incident, forgetting his many-sidedness, and the many other scenes, in which he faced death. As a man of letters he is well-nigh forgotten, although he wrote many histories, and a partial autobiography, wherein, with the modesty of a great soldier he told in vivid language of his perils and adventures. He was so modest in his first book, *The True Relation,* that he did not mention the Pocahontas incident, and one dry-as-dust antiquarian has seen fit from this omission to throw doubt on the story. Smith was so familiar with death that he might well omit to mention all his chance meetings with it. To him this was only a casual circumstance, a mere informal passing the time of day with Death, and no more worthy of a chronicle than any of the other thrilling encounters with the great destroyer. No one doubted the story in his life time, and many of his contemporaries have testified to it. Seemingly fearful that he might be charged with ingratitude, for making no record of it, in June, 1616, he addressed a letter to "The Most High, and Vertuous Princesses, Queene Anne of Great Brittanie," as follows:

> The loue I beare my God, my King and Countrie, hath so oft emboldened mee in the worst of extreme dangers, that now honestie doth constraine mee to presume thus farre beyond my selfe, to present your Maiestie this short discourse; if ingratitude be a deadly poyson to all honest vertues, I must bee guiltie of that crime if I should omit any

meanes to be thankfull. So it is, that some ten yeeres agoe, being in Virginia, and taken prisoner by the power of Powhatten their chiefe King, I receiued from this great Saluage exceeding great courtesie, especially from his sonne Nantaquas, the most manliest, comeliest, boldest spirit, Ieuer saw in a Saluage, and his sister, Pocahontas, the King's most deare and wel-beloued daughter, being but a childe of twelue or thirteene yeeres of age, whose compassionate pitifull heart, of my desperate estate, gaue me much cause to respect her. I being the first Christian, this proud King and his grim attendants euer I saw; and thus enthralled in their barbarous power, I cannot say I felt the least occasion of want that was in the power of those my mortall foes to preuent, notwithstanding all their threats. After some six weeks fatting among those Saluage Courtiers, at the minute of my execution, she hazarded the beating out of her owne brains to saue mine; and not only that, but so preuailed with her father that I was safely conducted to Iames towne; where I found about eight and thirtie miserable poore and sicke creatures to keepe possession of all those large territories of Virginia; such was the weakness of this poore Commonwealth, as had the Saluages not fed vs, we directly had starued. And this reliefe, most gracious Queene, was commonly brought vs by this Lady Pocahontas.

The Indian Princess fed the colonists and warned them of plots against them. Finally she came at a later day after Smith had gone to Europe, and they told her he was dead. She then married an English gentleman by the name of Rolf. Smith met her after her marriage and at first she was cool and would not speak. As he tells of this meeting:

But not long after she began to

talke, and remembered mee well what courtesies shee had done, saying, You did promise Powhatan what was yours should bee his and hee the like to you; you called him father being in his land a stranger, and by the same reason so must I doe you; which though I would have excused, I durst not allow of that title, because she was a King's daughter; with a well set countenance she said, Were you not afraid to come into my father's Countrie, and caused feare in him and all his people [but mee] and feare you here I should call you father; I tell you then I will, and you shall call mee childe, and so I will bee for euer and euer your Countrieman. They did tell vs alwaies you were dead, and I knew no other until I came to Plimoth.

From this it would seem that but for a chance estrangement, Smith would not have lived and died a bachelor. Although the dust has gathered upon his fame, he was not unhonoured in his own day. His companions in peril and his friends in England, have given him unstinted praise. Some of them marred eulogy, by putting his praises into verse, and we are compelled to say that none of them were poets. They entered into a poetical conspiracy of great magnitude against the beloved one. This is probably a sure certificate of fame, for no man can truly be called great until admiring worshippers have written poetry about him. It is true that many men of small figure come to this favour, but they make fine verse only a grotesque pleasantry— a tinsel sword and crown. But mere doggerel gains a dignity when it is spent in eulogy of real greatness, as the manhood of Ulysses shone through his rags and dignified them when he returned to his own hall. Bad as they are, I consider these loving eulogists worthy of some mention. R. Braithwait indites his verse, "To my worthy friend, Captain Iohn Smith." In this he alludes to:

Tragabigzanda, Callamata's love,
Deare Pocahontas, Madam Shanoi's too.

I take the liberty of suggesting that for "Callamata's love," we read "Calamity's love," believing that this is only another form of naming the Turkish Princess, and does not mean another love, and that this line lost its real meaning in the transcription. But what shall be said of "Madam Shanoi's too?" and was she another love, and was Smith a soldier of many loves? This being the only record of Madam Shanoi, she will have to be dismissed as an unimportant personage, and a mere casual intrusion into history. It is quite evident that we are warranted in maintaining that Smith's real loves like those of kings, made history, and when they did not do this they were the merest ephemera of the affections. Braithwait concludes with:

> And I could wish [such wishes would
>   doe well,]
> Many such Smiths in this our Israel.

Anthony Fereby, begins his verse: "To my noble brother and friend." He says:

> * * * for what deservedly
> With thy lifes danger, valour, pollicy,
> Quaint warlike stratagems, abillity
> And Judgement, thou has got, fame sets
>   so high
> Detraction cannot reach; thy worth shall
>   stand
> A patterne to succeeding ages. * * *

Tuissimus Ed. Jorden, addresses his verse "To his valiant and deserving friend." His eulogy closes thus:

> Good men will yeeld thee praise; then
>   sleight the rest;

> Tis best praise-worthy to have pleased the best.

Richard James, speaks of his:

> Deare noble Captaine, who by Sea and Land,
> To act the earnest of thy name hast hand
> And heart; * * *

Ma. Hawkins achieves the worst poetry, opening with the thrilling line:

> Thou that hast had a spirit to flie like thunder.

Richard Meade inquires in a burst of poetical emotion:

> Will not thy Country yet reward thy merit,
> Nor in thy acts and writings take delight?

In his closing line Edward Ingham avers that:

> Reader 'tis true; I am not brib'd to flatter,

as if his poetry were not evidence enough on this point.

M. Cartner says:

> But verse thou need 'st not to expresse thy worth.

He compares Smith to the famed Ithacan, and so also do I. C., and C. P., two unnamed eulogists who take a strong classical vein. Brian O'Rourke with true Hibernian splendour of diction begins with this line:

> To see bright honour sparkled all in gore.

Salo. Tanner says:

> Let Mars and Nepture both with pregnant wit,
> Extoll thy due deserts, Ile pray for it.

Smith offered to lead the Pilgrim Fathers to America in 1619, but the mission was denied him because he was not a Puritan. He died in 1631, having spent the last years of his life in authorship. His accounts of his life and explorations on this continent are filled with historical facts of real value. He was not too much of an historian to disdain small things, and even gives the names of his comrades and fellow colonists. This method of writing history puts the thrill of human life into what he relates. One cannot help but feel a friendly interest in the Wests, the Russells, the Burtons, the Bradleys, and the Walkers, and many others of familiar sound, for these are the names of people all about you. You find yourself wondering whether Burton, your shoemaker, is a descendant of the early adventurer, and whether Russell, your surgeon, derived any of his skill by inheritance from a soldier ancestor, who went out with Smith, and did his carving with the sword. As old Fuller quaintly says in like case, taking as his text, the discovery of a Hastings among the peasantry on the Earl of Huntingdon's estate:

> And I have reason to believe, that some who justly own the surnames and blood of Bohuns, Mortimers and Plantaganets [though ignorant of their

own extractions,] are hid in the heap of common people, where they find that under a thatched cottage which some of their ancestors could not enjoy in a leaded castle—contentment, with quiet and security.

The painted walking sticks who become cabinet ministers, the accidents of birth who become kings and the accidents of politics who become presidents, who infest the pages of history with a dessicated and puerile immortality, cut but a sorry figure when aligned with a manhood like this great captain's. The Genius of Platitude and Palaver has tried in vain to make them great; he is great because he has done the things, and no man ever spoke better of his deeds than the truth would bear. An English scholar, who has compiled his work, says of him:

> One cannot read the following Works without seeing that John Smith was

something more than a brave and experienced soldier. Not only in his modesty and self restraint, his moderation and magnanimity, his loyalty to the King, affection for the Church, and love for his Country, did he represent the best type of the English Gentleman of his day; but he was also a man of singular and varied ability. * * * It is not too much to say that had not Captain Smith of Willoughby, strove, fought and endured as he did, the present United States of America might never have come into existence.

A pleasing eulogy to read is that of two of the survivors of the "starving time," of the Virginia colony, as it was called. They thus testified to his worth:

* * * that in all his proceedings made justice his first guide and experience his second; ever hating baseness, sloth, pride and indignity, more

than any dangers; that never allowed more for himself than for his soldiers with him; that upon no danger would send them where he would not lead them himself; that would never see us want what he either had, or could by any means get us; that would rather want than borrow, or starve than not pay; that loved actions more than words, and hated falsehood and cozenage more than death; whose adventures were our lives and whose loss our deaths.

But the best key to his character is found in his written works. There in simple words that can charm little children, this faithful heart is recorded. In one burst of retrospect, he says:

Having been a slave to the Turks, prisoner amongst the most barbarous Salvages, after my deliverance commonly discovering and ranging those large rivers and unknowne Nations with such a handfull of ignorant companions that the wiser sort often gave mee up for lost, alwayes in mutinies, wants and miseries, blowne up with gunpowder; a long time prisoner among the French Pyrats, from whom escaping in a little boat by my selfe, and adrift all such a stormy winter night when their ships were split, more than a hundred thousand pounds lost, they had taken at sea, and most of them drowned on the Ile of Ree, not farr from whence I was driven ashore in my little boat, &c. And many a score of the worst of winter moneths lived in the fields; yet to have lived neere 37 yeares in the midst of wars, pestilence and famine, by which many hundred thousand have died about mee, and scarce five living of them that went first with mee to Virginia; and yet to see the fruits of my labours thus well begin to prosper; though I have but my labour for my pains, have I not much reason both privately and publikely to acknowledge it and give God thankes, whose omnipotent power onely delivered me, to doe the utmost of my best to make his name knowne in those remote parts of the world, and his loving mercy to such a miserable sinner.

Again he says:—

Who can desire more content that hath small meanes; or but only his merit to aduance his fortune, then to tread and plant that ground hee hath purchased by the hazzard of his life? If he haue but the taste of virtue and magnanimitie, what to such a minde can bee more pleasant, than planting and building a foundation for his Posteritie, gotte from the rude earth by God's blessing and his owne industrie, without prejudice to any? If hee haue any graine of faith or zeale in Religion, what can hee doe lesse hurtfull to any, or more agreeable to God; then to seeke to conuert those poore Saluages to know Christ and humanitie, whose labours with discretion will triple requite thy charge and paines? What so truely suites with honour and honestie, as the discouering things unknowne? erecting Townes, peopling Countries, informing the ignorant, reforming things vniust, teaching virtue; and gaine to our Native mother-countrie a kingdom to attend her; finde imployment for those that are idle, because they know not what to doe; so farre from wronging any, as to cause Posteritie to remember thee and remembering thee euer honour that remembrance with praise? * * * Then seeing we are not borne for our selues, but each to helpe other, and our abilities are much alike at the houre of our birth and the minute of our death; Seeing our good deedes, or our badde, by faith in Christ's merits, is all we haue to carrie our soules to heauen, or hell; Seeing honour is our liues ambition; and our ambition after death to haue an honourable memorie of our life; and seeing by noe meanes wee would bee abated of the dignities and glories of our predecessors; let vs imitate their vertues, to bee worthily their successors.

Sleep great Captain in your humble grave—you who were thrice worthy to be laid 'beside great kings at Westminister. No grave of England's dead holds more kingly dust than yours. We have read your story as you and your companions in arms have set it down. It is a tale of many lands and many peoples, of life eloquent and glorious. It brings us close to you and makes three hundred years seem but as a day. We have walked beside you as with satchel and shining morning face you crept, like snail, unwillingly to school. We have seen your hermitage in the woods of Lincolnshire where you took the queen's deer, and communed with Marcus Aurelius, dreaming of greatness like his. Dear to us is every passing fancy and every careless grace of that noble non-age. Dear and friendly are you as you lead us among the battle-fields of Europe, and through the perils that beset you. We have fearfully watched you careering down the lists at Regall to meet the flower of Turkish chivalry. We have felt your heart-throbs when the Turkish maiden made you a double captive, and we thought no ill of you that you honoured her love with your gratitude, and cherished her memory after many years had gone when you came to name the New World. Whether in school-boy cap and gown, or clad in mail, or naked in slavery, or bound before Powhattan awaiting his dreadful judgment, or watching and guarding Western Civilization in its very cradle-time, you were a man.

A DEFERRED CRITICISM
TO A POETESS OF PASSION

You in the Bohemia of newspaperdom, must be constantly reminded, as I am in other places, that the age of chivalry is not yet past. The pencil of the wandering hack-writer still does as much for the succor of distressed damsels seeking fame as did the lance of the ancient knight for his lady fair.

The lady lawyer, I use this term unadvisedly, argues her first case, and this becomes an event worthy of an admiring chronicle. The charms of toilet, the grace of manner, and the erudition of the fair Portia, are set forth with glowing eulogy. Young Briefless might argue twenty cases and not awaken half this interest. Perhaps if Portia would analyze the flattery offered her she might come to doubt whether it was entirely complimentary, and might feel that it carried with it a certain astonishment that a mere woman should do so well, instead of assuming this as a matter of course. But flattery is as immune from analysis on the part of the greedy, as sugar-plums. The new ways of the sex bring multiform embarrassments, and your critic has not the least of these. The aged professor and the young medico at the clinic and in the dissecting room hardly know how to harmonize their new relations towards the brave intruder upon their ways. Portia in the court room is apt to demand all things as belonging to her of hereditary right, and to concede as few obligations on her own part, as possible. The seasoned practitioner hardly knows how much satire or brute strength he may use to check her, or how much deference he should show her when he finds her tempted into trickery or pettifogging. So he shuffles and temporizes and evades responsibility, and saves his thunderbolts for the next bout with his learned brother.

One cannot object to the emancipation of sex, but can fairly object to the self conscious way in which the emancipation goes on. The demands upon our attention by women who are admitted to the bar, or who write books, or turn politicians, or practice medicine, or do the other things that seem novelties to them, has become a bore. It is not necessary that these pioneers should be eternally calling attention to the fact that they are women. Men do all of these things, and, heaven knows, are vain enough about it, but they do them without the air of saying "You see, I am only a man, and yet I can do this." May we not be allowed to yet look on women as a part of the great human family and not as a distinct species?

Although literature is not a new field for women, yet the consciousness of sex follows them there, and becomes the worst of hypertrophied mental tissue. I cannot find that "violet-weaving, pure, sweet-smiling Sappho," was thus afflicted, and it is now nearly three thousand years since she sang of love. So we must now be in a time of retrogression. These prefatory observations concluded, I am presumptious enough to think that I can, without violating the proper canons of gallantry suggest some reasons which may cause you to refrain from further poetical activity along certain lines.

Some trespass on gallantry should be pardoned, for gallantry in our sex has been the bane of your life. It has spoiled any promise you may have shown in earlier years. I remember when you were first putting forth your maiden efforts in verse. They were good enough rhymes to be published in the cross-roads weekly free of charge. It is true, as even you must admit, that if you thought them poetry you were more self-flattered than Mercutio. They were just plain rhymes; little jingles, and sometimes little jangles. I have tried to give them no dull-eared search, yet I cannot find a single line in them that is really yours that rings with music and power. However, if your verse had been simply of woods, and hills, and streams, and summer days, and blossoming flowers, you would have lived unknown to the great world, although you might have been the queen of letters at the cross-roads. But your constituency would have been limited by the subscription list of the cross-roads weekly. Whether by accident or design you struck other than bucolic themes and opened a vein of most amatory verse, and this advertised you because it was excessively amatory. You also met a lot of good fellows, both young and old in the newspaper world. They are always lion hunters, eager to make new finds, and gallant and quick to extend help to the latest female immigrant into Bohemia. They gave you the freedom of the kingdom in two-column laudation. They bade Flattery play you silvery airs and agreed that you should be heralded as a poet. They puffed your poems, and, gross and palpable though it was, you sickened not, but under this inspiration only ground out more. They announced your goings and your comings, and varied the monotony of their efforts to give you fame by occasionally announcing that you were about to be married to a distinguished gentleman, to whom, with their light and playful fancy, they attached great place in wealth or position. When a mere man journeys from place to place, the gleaners for the press do not always attend upon him, unless, indeed, he should happen to be a murderer or some other person of equal importance. But if you should happen to make a metropolitan visit, Genial Jenkins would be rapping at your boudoir door within half an hour after your arrival. Then as surely follows this interview which I take from next morning's *Daily Bangle:*

> The reporter for the *Bangle* met with a pleasant reception last evening from the beautiful Poetess of Passion in her charming Boudoir at the Auditorium. She wore a pale green tea-gown which showed

to decided advantage her petite and symetritical figure. Your reporter caught the merest tantalizing glimpse of a white satin slipper, together with its contents, peeping from the wondrous tea-gown. The softly shaded electric light shed a langorous glamour over the sparkling eyes and dimpled cheeks of the poetess.

"May I ask what literary work you are now engaged on?" I said, after I had been cordially greeted.

"O, I have concluded to write a novel of the Present, which will also be a novel of the Future," said the poetess. "It will be in the highest form *fin de siecle*. I shall give a realistic picture of the young man of the present day with all his vices. It has been said so often by the critics in this country and Europe that I could only excel in verse and especially in the poetry of the passions, that I shall now produce something worthy in prose, for I have really achieved all the fame I care for in poetry."

Of course this is quoted from memory and I cannot give the literal rendering of the blank form used for these many interviews. But you have a surer authority; turn to your scrap-book of newspaper clippings about yourself and you will find this interview there, tea-gown, slippers and all. They are ancient stage properties of yours, although, of late years they have had a diminishing use. But puffing counts in the long run; it makes prime ministers as well as poets. You had some commendation that was honest enough even though it was shallow. Some of the people whose good opinion you should have valued and respected, refused to read your poetry; others read it with indignation, and others refused to consider it seriously either for good or bad, but treated it with broad humor and blunt wit, and your muse as of the *opera bouffe* order.

Slowly the deference of the press for you has become rather third class with a tinge of good-natured contempt in it. The newspaper brethren like fine titles and second names for every public character. They do not permit any Mavericks on their range, and like to put their own brand on the herds they round up from far and near. When you have been in their eye long enough in one capacity they fix a name on you. So they created the Sweet Singer of Michigan, and the Poet of the Sierras. To you they gave the name of Poetess of Passion, and joyed in its euphony. You have been one of their Cherry Sisters, and they have accorded you a mock deference, thinly disguised as real. It must be difficult some of the time to determine whether the flowers they throw at you are cabbages or roses; superficially, they might be either. You can hardly get much of a review now, no matter how burns the lava tide of your verse. You have become a stock figure as much as The Grand Old Man, or The Langtry Lily, and you do not need description or explanatory notes, or an introduction. Your epitomization is embodied in Poetess of Passion. But these are horizon fancies, and I want to look into the near-by heavens.

I have a copy of your Red Book, called *Poems of Passion*. A wilder fancy than mine would suggest that the blushing cover was stirred by what it covered. The preface alone is worth all the labour of reading the book; it is a delicious bit of egotism that cannot be duplicated anywhere. In its opening sentence you say:

> Among the twelve hundred poems that have emanated from my too-prolific

pen, there are some forty or fifty which treat entirely of that emotion which has been denominated "the grand passion, love." A few of these are of an extremely fiery character.

Then you proceed to state that you had issued a prior book of verse from which you had omitted these fiery sonnets. Now you describe how you were called to account for this most laudable expurgation, thus:

> But no sooner was the book published than letters of regret came to me from all parts of the globe, asking why this or that love-poem was omitted. These regrets were repeated to me by so many people, that I decided to collect and issue these poems in a small volume to be called *Poems of Passion.*

This picture of "friends and strangers in all parts of the globe," crying out for their loved ones among your love-poems, is more affecting than authentic. It is impossible for the healthy mind to even imagine their grief. One would like to see these devotees of passion; they would doubtless present some curious, if not instructive anthropological studies. Did these bitter disappointments well up in Thibetan Polyandry, or by the Bosphorus, or on the shore of Great Salt Lake, or where that other community of Passion Worshippers taints the air of the Empire State? One cannot locate elsewhere, any large collection of those who are ruled by Her of the Hydra Head. You confess with strange pride to the authorship of twelve hundred poems. The magnitude of your score has tempted me to investigate other poets to see if they make up your sum. Keats wrote fifty poems, Hood seventy-six, Burns six hundred and fifty, and Tom Moore about the same; Bryant, fifty, Tennyson about three hundred and fifty, Pope, one hundred and sixty, Wordsworth about eight hundred, and Mrs. Hemans two hundred and fifty. Surely these figures will still further serve to increase the appreciation your admirers have for your poems. One may be allowed to guess that those admirers are found pretty exclusively among men who have dealt in lumber or pork with but little time for literature. This sort of a business man is apt to imagine that if a poem is not positively bad in all ways, and if the mere externals of poetry have been attended to, it is real poetry and not a clever counterfeit. In the fruitfulness of your muse you excel all the great names of English literature. It may possibly be said that these figures are compiled from merely published poems and that there are others not published. If you could have considerately refrained in like manner we should not now have twelve hundred publicly announced poems. You have evidently lisped in numbers for the numbers came, although your numbers, unlike most of Pope's are of a mathmatical-amorous sort. This standard compels us to measure poetical greatness as certain loyal Americans do national greatness—as if it were a matter of barrels of pork and bushels of wheat. Thus our Western Muse scorns her barren European sister. You consider it necessary to explain some of the poems in this book and to show why they were written, and in doing this you hint, not too obscurely, that they were inspired by some experiences that have come under your own observation. You also explain that the most amorous of these verses have not so bad a meaning as the superficial reader might impute to them. Now this explanation only accentuates the prevelant suspicion that these poems are irretrievably bad. With delicate naivete you say of one of them:

Delilah was written and first published in 1877. I had been reading history and became stirred by the power of such women as Aspasia and Cleopatra over such grand men as Anthony, Socrates and Pericles. Under the influence of this feeling I dashed off *Delilah*, which I meant to be an expression of the powerful fascination of such a woman upon the memory of a man, even as he neared the hour of death. If the poem is immoral, then the history which inspired it is immoral. I consider it my finest effort.

Now if this poem is a good poem people don't care how you came to write it. Your fame is too new and garish to warrant any excessive curiosity on that score. Nor did the public need to be told that you "dashed off *Delilah*." It is characteristic of the young poet to "dash off" his poems (in prefaces). It gives one an air of verve and fire, and careless excess of power to "dash off" these rough patterns, and makes one's muse like swift Camilla scour the plain. You say that if the poem is immoral, the history that inspired it is immoral. "The history that inspired it,"—aye, there's the rub; that history *is* immoral. Aspasia and Cleopatra are not characters out of a Sunday-school book. Socrates was a loose fish, and Pericles was no better than he should be, and we must not confound Mark Anthony with Saint Anthony. It may be of no significance, but I find no poem in my Red Book speaking forth the woes of the wife in these ancient marital difficulties. If Zanthippe could have her epic, it might show how it was that she lost her temper and became the jest of the centuries on account of trouble over that woman Aspasia. As for Mrs. Pericles, she was probably a poor little mouse of a woman, living a decent humble life, and not worth comparing with that grand creature, Aspasia—certainly not worth a nineteenth century poem of passion. I think that Mrs. Cæsar and Mrs. Anthony, could tell us some things if they had a fit chronicler, either in prose or verse, that would demoralize the halo which poetesses of passion have placed round the heads of those "grand characters." You complete your confession as to this poem by stating that you consider it your "finest effort." This practice of battering yourself with boquets has something so colossally egotistical about it, that the critic, supposed to be used to the worst cases, gasps for breath. Returning to our text, I quote the finest lines of this finest effort of yours:

She smiles—and in mad tiger fashion,
As a she-tiger fondles her own,
I clasp her with fierceness and passion,

And kiss her with shudder and groan.

And here is some more from *Ad Finem*, which you say is another of the poems which have been condemned so much:

> I know in the way that sins are reckoned,
> This thought is a sin of the deepest dye;
> But I know too, that if an angel beckoned,
> Standing close to the throne on High,
> And you, adown by the gates infernal,
> Should open your loving arms and smile,
> I would turn my back on things supernal,
> To lie on your breast a little while.
>
> To know for an hour you were mine completely—
> Mine in body and soul, my own—
> I would bear unending tortures sweetly,
> With not a murmur and not a moan.

Another of the Great Condemned is *Communism* and in this you express yourself thus:

And on nights like this when my blood runs riot
With the fever of youth and its mad desires,
When my brain in vain bids my heart be quiet,
When my breast seems the center of lava-fires,
Oh, then is the time when most I miss you,
And I swear by the stars, and my soul, and say,
That I would have you and hold you, and kiss you,
Though the whole world stands in the way.

And like Communists, mad and disloyal,
My fierce emotions roam out of their lair;
They hate King Reason for being loyal—
They would fire his castle, and burn him there.
O love, they would clasp you, and crush you, and kill you,

In the insurrection of uncontrol,
Across the miles, does this wild war
  thrill you
That is raging in my soul.

As for your *Conversion* it is so Swinburnish, or Whitmanish that I desire not to give it, having what you have not, a fear of the repressive rules of the United States postal department against aiding in the dissemination of a certain kind of literature. In the title to this poem you have stolen the very altar cloth and dyed it scarlet. Of what avail is this lawless, wanton, verse? It bears the stigmata of mental debauchery and hysteria and does not teach one valuable lesson. To the psychopathist it may possess a curious scientific interest; but to laymen this demented verse is as abhorrent as the maunderings of a maniac. If it does express the language of a human heart is it not better that that language should remain untranslated, or at least that it should have no such brutal translation? Even poets who have compelled us to print expurgated editions of their poetry do not vapour in such trite eroticism as this. In some instances Burns wrote for the ale-house, evidently to win the applause of his pot-companions; it is vulgar enough too, but little redeemed by his splendid genius. But you nowhere find him afflicted with hysteria. Plain common vulgarity and coarseness carries its own antidote against harm. But Burns held the sacred things sacred from poetical defilement. There is no taint in these lines:

> Thou ling'ring star with less'ning ray,
> That lov'st to greet the early morn,
> Again thou ush'rest in the day
> My Mary from my soul was torn.
>
> *　　*　　*
>
> The golden hours on angel wings
> Flew o'er me and my dearie.

My love is like the red, red rose
Just newly sprung in June.
   *   *   *

Had we never loved sae blindly,
Had we never loved sae kindly,
Never met, or never parted,
We had n'er been broken-hearted.
   *   *   *

Fare thee wee'l thou first and fairest,
Fare thee wee'l thou best and dearest.

 Do you find in the great Scottish poet of the affections any trace of that tigerish affection, that howls for its tiger mate, through your poems? Civilized love is not a beast raging rampantly abroad seeking whom it may devour. It is not a vampire or a vulture that claws and tears and drinks warm blood on occasion. It is decent and fair to look upon, and does not say to flaming youth—Let virtue be as wax and melt in her own fire. It goes with the bride in her happy innocence to the altar; it guards and purifies the mother's heart as she watches over her children; it makes the dullest and homeliest life, noble and kindly; it follows to the end, and through life's last and greatest affliction it clings in dearest remembrance to the departed spirit beyond the confines of the grave. It has no affinity for that raging fever which you grow eloquent over. The great alienists would find something familiar in your verse. For such manifestations they have a name—Sadism. Here are some specimens of this poetic abandon from the German philosopher, Nietzsche.

> The splendid beast raging in its lust after prey and victory. Do your pleasure ye wantons; roar for very lust and wickedness. The path to one's own heaven ever leads through the voluptousness of one's own hell. How comes it that I have yet met no one * * * who knew morality as a problem, and this

problem as his personal distress, torment, voluptousness, passion?

You have few noble words to relieve these darker passages—in fact your other verse seems but a setting for them. Whittier said of Burns:

> And if at times an evil strain,
> To lawless love appealing,
> Broke in upon the clear refrain
> Of pure and healthful feeling,
>
> It died upon the eye and ear
> No inward answer gaining;
> No heart had I to see or hear
> The discord and the staining.

This loving eulogist tells what every heart must feel. The Burns of the ale-house was also the Burns of Bonnie Doon and Afton Water, of the Cotter's Hearth, and Highland Mary. The vulgar line which comes now and then is but a passing shadow cast lightly on this shining gold of love and honour and plighted troth, and all the hearthstone deities. Your poems of peaceful refuge are too small and too few to give us safe escape from the surging riot that fills your Red Book. When you aim at a restful poem you are bound to make it a thing of silly gush and affectation, as like real emotion as that depicted by the painted, shrill voiced belle of the music-hall stage. Lovers named Guilo, Lippo, Beppo, and Romney, and one by the Christian name of Paul, are the subjects of the lighter and less gustatory strokes of your prolific pen. Thus does your muse make eyes at the audience through the paint and tinsel:

Yes, yes, I love thee, Guilo; thee alone,
Why dost thou sigh and wear that face of
  sorrow?

So I loved Romney? Hush thou foolish one—
I should forget him wholly, wouldst thou
  let me;

A DEFERRED CRITICISM

Or but remember that his day was done
From that most supreme hour when first
    I met thee.
And Paul? Well, what of Paul? Paul
    had blue eyes,
And Romney gray, and thine are darkly
    tender.
One finds fresh feelings under change of
    skies—
A new horizon brings a newer splendour.

You play this tune with variations; here is another form:

Why art thou sad my Beppo? But last eve,
Here at my feet, thy dear head on my
    breast,
I heard thee say thy heart would no more
    grieve,
Or feel the old ennui and unrest.

What troubles thee? Am I not all thine
    own—
I, so long sought, so sighed for and so
    dear?

And do I not live but for thee alone?
Thou has seen Beppo, whom I loved last year.

Thou art not first? Nay, and he who would be
Defeats his own heart's dearest purpose then.
No surer truth was ever told to thee,
Who has loved most, the best can love again.

If Lippo, [and not he alone] has taught
The arts that please thee, wherefore art thou sad
Since all my vast love-lore to thee is brought?
Look up and smile my Beppo, and be glad.

This apish verse, coined in the cheap and vulger similitude of Italian love-making, soft and langorous, breathing of orange groves and summer nights, with its thees and thous put in to hide its verbal poverty, must have been thought poetry by you or it would not be in the Red Book. According to this, life in order to be at its happiest must consist of a quick succession of casual, yet tigerish love affairs, the more the merrier and the more the better. This gospel may do for the man-about-town, and for his compatriots in the half-world, but it will hardly do to bring up a family on. This verse looks easy and tempting; it fires your critic into parodistic emulation. Here are some verses which suffer in the same way, "tossed off," of course:

> My Beppo why dost thou complain,
> Thou hast my this year's kisses;
> Lippo was my last year's swain,
> He took those last year's blisses.
> Why task me for a thing forgot,
> When this year I am all thine own,
> That happy past remember not,
> When me its bliss long since has flown.

The ragbags of the past disclose
One tangled web of silken skein
Which other hands than thine have wove,
But which thy own must weave again.

Let loves be new and ever range,
Scorning dull-ey'd Satiety,
Hunting content in change on change,
And pleasure in variety.

And so we take leave of the Red Book—a book which contains no reason for having been written.

AMERICAN NOTES

It was many and many a year ago—for so the account should run with us who have seen fast history-making, that Dickens came over the sea to look at England's First-born. The brat was lusty, raw and ungainly, full of strange oaths, bumptious, arrogant and a braggart. These qualities made its parentage easily recognizable, and yet gave great offense to its kinsman. Being of the same blood, perhaps he should have treated the faults of extreme youth more kindly, yet time softens resentments, and we can now afford to laugh over the follies of our whelp-age. He hurt our feelings terribly in *Martin Chuzzlewit* and *American Notes*, yet despite the pain of wounded vanity we took him into favour again. Those who loved him tried to condone his guilt by attributing it to British bull-headedness and ignorance.

There is a strong suspicion now extant that there were Americans a few decades since, who were as narrow, insular and provincial as the John Bulls themselves. Our average is better now, and still we have something to mend. General Choke and Jefferson Brick are no longer with us, but we have their modifications in the more refined, self-styled Intense American. He has established the Thirty-second Degree of Americanism, infested by his class alone. Still, his vagaries are mild and innocuous. Sometimes they are manifested in a desire to run the

American Flag up in all parts of the landscape, and I have expected that he would eventually adorn every corn-crib and smoke-house in the land with it. He has a theory that the daily and hourly use of the Flag increases patriotism. Jacob with his device of the peeled twigs for increasing the number of his flocks, was not more cunning than our Professional Patriot with his devices for increasing the number of Patriots in this country. To the American who carries his patriotism in his heart and not on his sleeve, his country's flag tells more eloquently than printed page or martial song, of American valour—of brave men and brave deeds. If it be a standard scarred and torn in battle, the whole earth holds no inspiration like it. But he does not need the aid of artificial excitants to make him love his country and her flag.

Recently an ex-president has come

forward with some new renditions of Flag-Service. This fresh pattern of patriotism is announced by the fortunate magazine that secured it—at great expense—thus:

> It was * * * idea that the stars and stripes should float over every school house in America. Now in a stirring article he carries the idea further and shows why the flag should find a place over every fireplace in our country; what it would mean to future generations, and why the flag should appeal to every woman.

We are further informed that "the article will rank with the author's most eloquent public utterances." As much as we respect ex-presidents, we cannot avoid suspicion that this promised mine of rich eloquence has been "salted" in the advertisement. Commonplace at a dollar a line is too dear, even when it is the commonplace of an ex-president.

There are living American women who have been taught patriotism in a sterner school than the Great American Kindergarten for Women. They cannot gain new inspiration from pedagogical and dilletant patriotism, addressed to a magazine constituency assumed to be in its milk teeth. The Firesides are not clamouring to be fed new rations of spoon-vicutals by Eminent Hands. This nursery employment does not suggest a fit answer to the common, vacuous query, "what shall we do with our ex-presidents?" Let us rather continue to employ them for periodical deliverances of other platitudes whose prosperity lies in our acutely adoring ears.

With all the decadence among the followers of General Choke and Jefferson Brick they still have a stifled sneer for the migratory American, acknowledging ancestral fealty to the great mother-land of nations, if he shall buy a pair of trousers in London. One of the minor regulations of the Intense American is that you must not travel in foreign lands, or at least only do so under apology, before you "have seen all there is to see in your own country." You must inspect the colorless waste between Saco and Waco as a condition precedent to foreign travel. Our Intense American may be said to be in his richest vein when he detects the harmless and necessary immigrant to these shores bringing out the flag of his native land on some fete day. Only a call for troops will suffice for this treason. I do not forget that I first learned from Jefferson Brick of the Curse of British Gold, and how it was being used to corrupt the free American electorate. Originally it was the hideous Cobden Club that was distributing this gold, and thereafter and more recently the Money Kings of Lombard Street. From this same well of patriotism I learned that before we adopt national policies we ought to find out what England wants us to do, and then not do it. Upon these activities the bunting trust thrives, and the voice of our hustings becomes a mere hysterical echo of the patriot cannon at Bunker Hill.

Since Dickens was with us in 1841 many things have come to pass that the Muse of History with her large disdain for trifles has made no note of. She only records the big events in her tiresome folios and never descends to chronicling small beer. The real life of human kind has been left to gossips like Pepys, who have saved for us the tattle of the tea parties and the coffee houses. While the Gibbons have been telling in sonorous phrase of camps and courts, these humble chatterers have remained unemulous, telling trifling tales. They cared not a button about the dress parades of kings, nor were they fearsome of posterity. They thought it important to set down what they ate and drank, what they wore, what physic they took and how they dressed themselves or quarreled with their neighbours, or amused themselves on yesterday. The trial of the Seven Bishops will not lack a historian, but we must look to these gleaners of little sheaves, if we wish to know what Hodge was doing, or how 'Arry and 'Arriet spent their holidays in the English meadows in the year 16—. There is a suggestion in this for modest chroniclers of our own time, who are willing to wait two hundred years for fame. As topics for these little histories I would suggest in passing:

The Rise and Fall of the Crazy Quilt.

The Age of Plush.

The Influence of Pie on National Character.

The Moral Aspect of Tidies.
The Strange Career of the Pillow Sham.

Disquisitions on these subjects, sagely written would in time become as valuable as those of the older *Tattlers* and *Spectators*. I consider that My Lady Lizzard's Tucker, and the gentle follies of Clarinda and Bubalina, as worthy of a memoir as the stilted performances of a fat-witted prime minister.

Dickens saw us before we had stolen Texas or the Empire of the Golden Gate from poor Mexico. It was before the Argonauts of '49 had commenced to thread the buffalo trails over the plains and to hunt the passes of the Sierras. Our line of expansion was into the fever-and-ague belt of the Mississippi Valley. The City of Eden in Martin Chuzzlewitt was undoubtedly a much exaggerated caricature of the reality, just as Bumble the beadle, the Parish Workhouse, or Doctor Squeers' School were exaggerations. But in none of these would you have the least trouble in finding the original. Jefferson Brick and General Choke and the New York Daily Sewer and the Rowdy Journal, were not all a myth. The criticism of Dickens touched us where we were most sensitive. We always had an inner feeling that slavery was an abomination. We dimly saw that in its atrocities, the fifth century lived again and mocked at number nineteen—the great pharisee of the centuries. Dickens came from a nation whose war-ships had patrolled the African coast in crushing the slave trade, when this century was young. Through our assertiveness and Fourth of July declamation, we must have felt that our nation was yet unripe and that our morals might be bettered. Hence our anger when the exposed nerve was touched by our kinsman.

Our jingoes were offensive and truculent and they could smell the blood of an Englishman at a considerable distance, and long for it. They wreaked a ruder and more brutal vengeance on the Lion, than now, and the spleen and hatred engendered by two wars was invigorated by the presence of the crippled veterans of the Revolution who were disposed on all Fourth of July platforms. So buoyant and joyous and obtuse was our national conceit that we saw no incongruity in prating of liberty and freedom, while we were holding millions of human beings in slavery. We furnished rare sport for a satirist like Dickens, who had never spared his own country a deserved gibe.

The genius which described the Circumlocution Office, the abuses of the courts, and the Parish Workhouses and

Charity Schools of England would naturally riot in the wealth of raw material found here. 'Tis a vain task to balance all the gains and losses of fifty years. It must be admitted that when Dickens first saw us we were somewhat imperfect in the use of the fork, and we ate our meals with such dispatch that one who sat at meat more than ten minutes was looked on as a person of sedentary habits. We frescoed the floors in public places with tobacco, and the hotel towel was the subject of frequent and acrimonious remark. Pie was still our national dish and dominated all more effete refections from Passamaquaddy to Carondelet.

Life in 1841 had some advantages however. The Fifth Empire of the Distended Hoop was still in the womb of Fashion. Women did not adorn their backs and heads with the monstrous pads of a later time. The Age of Plush had not yet arrived. The Japanese gewgaws, and Chinese decorative misfits, the hand-painted china and ceramic fads, the hideous tidies and inflammable strawstack lamp chimneys, and above all, the crazy quilt, were unknown. Woman partook of literature in those golden days by the simple method of sitting down and reading a book. She did not pursue Culture with a Club, bristling with constitutions and by-laws and presidents and vice-presidents and boards of directors and committees and a general hurrah and whirl of parliamentary practices. She did not chastise the Tyrant, Man, with the vigor recently shown. She did tatting, chrocheting and fancy work, and made samplers and penwipers and woolly dogs. If she was literary she wrote nice stories for whatever magazine was the embryonic *Ladies' Home Journal* of the time. She did not "wallow" in conventions and congresses then as now. It was a day when the sepulchral Best Room was the good housewife's shrine, and the what-not and the fair, round center-table, were her household gods.

If a reincarnated Dickens should return here, he might still find some food for satire. We should probably accept his corrective offices more kindly now in these days of close fraternization between the Lion and the Eagle. On the way over he would be sure to meet a young lady—one of Cook's, from Cherry Valley, Ill.,—who would pester him for his autograph. He would have to triple-plate himself in dogged British reticence to withstand the assaults of our indefatigable reporters. The Lotus Club or some other club would feast him, and smooth lawyers and well-fed brokers of a literary turn, would smother him with after-dinner adulation.

In his purblind British way he would seek to find out something about New York politics. He would see Platt and Croker in their busy whirls and would never be able to tell which was which. Among other reflections, he would conclude that this was the Age of Woman, and that this gentle metal was to take its place in the social formation with stone, and gold and iron. We have Womens' magazines and newspapers, and womens' corners, and womens' supplements to great dailies, and womens' clubs and conventions and congresses, and a woman's revision of the Bible, and a religious cult established by a woman, principally for women. The Pilgrim Mothers having been non-progressive in their day, a movement has been organized to rescue them from obscurity, and to compel equal mention for them with the Pilgrim Fathers. We have women doctors, and lawyers, and drummers and undertakers. We are industrously building up a separate literature for women, strictly antiseptic and free from coarse rude things. Letters are becoming Bokized—"male and female created He them." Perhaps the time will come when we have sufficiently segregated woman from the great human family, that it will be considered as improper for men and women to read each other's literature, as it is now for them to wear each other's clothes. The Expurgated Novel has appeared, evidently censored by the Order of Decayed Clergymen. Ladies' magazines are edited with the camera, and the kodac is mightier than the pen. The Genius of Tatting is at the helm. With all this favour to The Young Person, the newspaper still brings its daily muck of crime into our homes; although but lately Dickens' novels were excluded from a New England public library as immoral. Having once reaped so well in our field of folly, Dickens, if he could return would get good gleanings from the aftermath of that field.

But perhaps Dickens would be best charmed with Chicago—behemoth, biggest born of cities, the chief shrine in the Gospel of Bigness. Here, as in all other places where the soul of his unblest British feet should seek rest, he would be compelled to "see the town." This rite of American hospitality would not be omitted, either in Chicago, or Oshkosh, Kalamazoo or Topeka. No matter what the town was, or how little there was to see, he would have to undergo this supreme ordeal. He would have to go and gaze admiringly at factories and shops and other monuments to civic pride. Seeing the town in Chicago would certainly embrace the stockyards, where as the prideful native informs all strangers, they kill a hog a second, the year round. The reporters would give out that he was "very much impressed with Chicago." That is the way in Chicago; the traveler from Mars, the New Zealander, the man from poor old London, and from poorer old New York, is always "very much impressed," when he reaches Chicago.

If the wayfaring stranger is not apparently impressed offhand and at first blush, the priests of the Gospel of Bigness have this formula of attack. First inform him that Chicago has two millions of people, and that fifty years ago it was a village of log cabins. This ought to fetch him, but if it fail, then refer to the Chicago Fire, and to the New Chicago springing Phoenix-like from its ashes. If he be still stubborn-kneed, bring on the Stock Yards with its toll of death, or the tunnel under the lake—that wonder of the world twenty-five years ago. If he remain obdurate, the new thirty million dollar sewer may fetch him. If everything else fails, he must succumb to the World's Fair. This is Chicago's *chef-d'œuvre*. On this subject look out for the inquisitors, for if you have not seen this wonder, you will have meted to you supreme pity and contempt. You will be made to wish that the Fair had been swallowed up before you heard of it. However, this will not ease your pain, for ever after it would be spoken of as the greatest swallowing-up in history. Dickens would find the Great Fire still celebrated with rejoicings, and lurid woodcut flames in the newspapers. The Fire has really lost all the advantages it once had as a Public Calamity, but its fame for Bigness will endure forever. From the Chicago point of view, pity and contempt for New York rises to the sublime; the island city is a mere wart on the face of the earth.

It is a trait of municipal callowness to brag. London and Paris never yell their brags at one another. Their secure position does not need to be continually asserted. Let a journalistic wag in New York fling a grotesque gibe at Chicago and she arises in majesty and pours vitriol on her decrepit rival. I quote from memory a waggish leader on Chicago that appeared in a New York paper:

> As you approach Chicago, she becomes foully manifest by a dull, livid cloud that obscures the sky. You burst into this mephitic drapery, feeling as though you had tumbled into a sewer. * * * It is a common thing to see her merchant princes in their shirt sleeves sitting on the front porches of their palatial homes enjoying an evening smoke. * * * The knife-swallowing act can still be seen at the hotels. The

Gent flourishes in Chicago—it is his natural home. Few Chicago families have grandparents; they cannot afford to.

The Home Guards in Chicago took this waggery seriously. They asserted that Chicago was as good as anybody, and that her pedigree, sanitation and manners were A. 1.

These are the reflections of new readings of American Notes. If Dickens could come again, he would find a nation mellowed and ripened with the years. He would find that the old order had given way to the new. He would find cities provincial and rustic then, cosmopolitan now. He would find a national life and ambition broad and catholic, not narrow and jealous. He would find a nation that remembers slavery as a horrible dream is remembered in the clear light of mid-noon, a nation purified by war, and the long, smouldering embers of that war, dead and lifeless. He would find us able to laugh at the follies and vices he mocked. He would find the great republic of the west living in happy amity with its mother land, the old hatreds and bickerings gone forever.

AMERICANISM IN LITERATURE

The critic who ventures discussion of American literature, risks an encounter with the Intense American. The jurisdiction of this national policeman is to see that the patriotism of his countrymen suffers no diminution or abatement. Of late he has paid some attention to the literary part of his authority. He insists on running the American Flag up in the library, as a lightning rod to protect American authors from any chance thunderbolts of criticism. The British critic is especially warned to keep off the green growth of American letters. Our watchman's oath of allegiance to American authors, excludes loyalty to all others, and so he becomes an uncomfortable and uncompromising person. I have long wanted to criticise Longfellow for the didactic character of some of his poems, and the ticketed and labeled moral that is so often intruded. A good tale is often spoiled by the intrusive moral. If it were not rank treason I would like to say that Hiawatha as a poem is partly spoiled because of its form as a long monotonous chant in which the refrain of the unvariant lines is early worn out, and thenceforth becomes a weariness. We learn from the Intense American that some of our authors have Intense Americanism, that Bryant was a "thorough American," and that a "spirit of True Americanism breathes in Longfellow." These awe-inspiring terms not being defined, we may take them to be simply an exercise in phrase-mongering.

Perhaps after all, this True, this Thorough, this Intense Americanism, is simply a State of Mind, in which Patriotism uplifts itself into a seventh heaven by simply tugging at its boot-straps. The vocabulary of uncritical adulation in Europe does not seem to have an equivalent term. He would be a daring idolator indeed who should insist that Dickens, or Thackeray, or Reade were gifted with Intense Britishism, for they committed many treasons by attacking every British institution from the House of Lords down to the dinners of snobs. It is difficult to discover that Cervantes had True Castileanism, or Plato True Greceianism, or Dante True Italianism. Our own Brander Mathews has set us some lessons in literary patriotism, the humor of which seems unconscious on his part. Thus does he warn youngest readers against the deadly snare of British literature:

> It cannot be said too often or too emphatically that the British are foreigners, and that their ideals in life, in literature, in politics, in taste, in art, are not our ideals.

From this author we also learn that it is:

> In consequence of the wholesome Americanism imparted in the school room, that American boys and girls have increased their demand for American books.

Foolish Americans have always had the same weakness for foreign authors, that they have for foreign goods, and this unnatural appetite must be checked by authority. The sad admission must be made that it is too late to put a tariff on British brains—the serpent has

has already crept in. The dogberrys of our literary police will call out in the street, but despite their warnings, vagrom Englishmen will to some extent still commit breaches of our peace in prose and verse. I refuse to thrill over the spectacle of the American Youth becoming so infected with True Americanism of the Bander Mathews kind that he rapidly turns to American authors. If there is any one primal and unchanging element in the character of the American Youth, it is his disregard of the authors who write his books. Nor does he care very much about the exact *locus in quo* of his fiction. *Robinson Crusoe, The Swiss Family Robinson,* and *Tom Brown,* mean just as much to an American boy as to an English boy. Such books have no nationality; they are written for the universal boy. For like reasons the Eton boy could gloat over *Tom Sawyer* and *Huckleberry*

Finn, without disloyalty to the Crown.

So many of us Yankees are Jacobites at heart, drinking secretly to the king over the water; we find creative genius where we can, undeterred by the True American. Our nation drones through one generation in deadly peace, hearing no sound but that of mill and loom, and the pleasant tinkle of little verses. No minstrel of our own breaks the silence, but from across the seas comes a strain of daring music from England's new singer. The majestic *Recessional* has set her heart afire and made us wish that heaven would send us such a poet. This poem would have an equal appeal for the Pharaohs, for Moses and Aaron, for the nations of later times, that grow drunken with power. It has the measured majesty of the speech of the prophets when they foretold the doom of nations. It is a lost fragment from Jeremiah or Isaiah. It has a Scriptural eloquence, sonorous, uplifting, called from the clearer hill-tops to the valleys below. It is a battle hymn and also a hymn of peace for the time when battles are over. It seems to close the century with the sound we have been listening for. This singer surely does not belong to the puddering rout of birth-day ode-makers who periodically sing lullabys to the English people. Perhaps he stole his fire from strange lands where he wandered, loving every spot where there was a man alive. Was there some alchemy in the branding Indian sun that made his soul great so that he could stand stern-browed at England's jubilee and tell her in Homeric verse that all her pomp was one with Nineveh and Tyre? This psalm is his title deed to Westminster. None but he could smite the chords with might, as there was but one in that heroic test of long ago, who could bend the great bow of Ulysses and make the string "sound sweetly as the swallow's song." The lines of Coleridge seem meant for this music:

> And now 'twas like all instruments,
> Now like a lonely flute;
> And now it is an angel's song
> That makes the heavens be mute.

We would like to feel that he owed some debt to New England, where he tarried awhile, but it is plain that he is English to the core, a child of the Thames, and not of the Ganges or the Merrimac. A little later when our ambition was leaping ocean barriers he sobered us by telling how basely or how nobly we might bear *The White Man's Burden.*

Shall we shut any part of this inspiration from our ears because it did not come from the banks of the Hudson or the Mississippi? Could our army of flag-wavers with their artificial devices for manufacturing artificial patriotism, so move a great race? Meanwhile Brander Mathews and his constabulary will continue to pick their flints and fight Bunker Hill over again against the British invader.

The even-blooded American who does not care whether an author has the ingredient of True Americanism in his inkwell or not, will still claim free trade rights with British literature. Perhaps this weakness of Intense Americanism is responsible for the belief, current in certain quarters that *A Man Without a Country*, is a great romance. This patriotic sermon—this high class Fourth of July oration has been given the title of the Great American Story. It is really quite interesting and instructive for fifteen-year-olds. It is the history of a youth, who in a moment of silly pique, being nagged by his captors, said that he wished he might never hear of the United States again. This was only the bitter froth of his real sin, for he had intrigued with Aaron Burr against his country, and that fascinating traitor had woven him tight in his web. The Powers-That-Be could forgive the real treason, and let the head traitor go free, but they could not forgive the boy's petulant lack of lip service. So they sent him on the high seas, where he wandered for many weary years a remorseful derelict, and by great command he was never to hear his country spoken of. They adopted towards him an Americanized version of the punishment of the Wandering Jew and of Tantalus, until old age came and death relieved him of his pain. This is a pretty story with a moral as obvious as a mountain. Later editions of it are spoiled somewhat by the egotism of authorship, which impels Mr. Hale to explain that it is a myth, and his reasons for writing it and all about the lesson that it teaches. But the moral somewhat loses its flavour with the callowest youth, when he sees around him many patriots who wave the Old Flag with one hand while they reach for a fat appropriation or a swindling government contract with the other. Aaron Burr at least did not buy legislatures and boards of aldermen.

The moral seems to be, superficially, that to be immune, you need only shape your schemes for the destruction of the institutions of your country to the prevailing fashion. You can then found an orphan asylum or a great university, and the hats will fly off as you go by.

All this may be thought a by-path from books, but human life is stretched along the by-ways as well as along the main traveled roads. This preface brings to mind some Americans who have not made a strutting parade of their patriotism. In example of this we have such Americans as Lowell, whose patriotism and love of country had no dross upon it; whose scholarship was as broad and generous as the seas that wash our shores; who never penned provincial and rustic cant about True Americanism; who loved books as a man and not as an American, and who could love a book neither more nor less because of the nationality of the author; who held close fellowship with the great of every land without a thought that it made him any the less an American. With him the world of letters had no narrowing partition lines that could separate Shakespeare, Cervantes, and Moliere from Hawthorne and Poe and Emerson and make one less than the other. The dead who sleep at Westminster were his blood brothers. With him we can safely place Irving, Hawthorne, Poe and Holmes. The fame of these rests on their genius and not on the accident of nationality. The many influences that may have somewhat dwarfed American scholarship, have not modified Lowell's genius. He would have honoured any land. As a poet and essayist he had a ripened wit and learning that places him as the first of American scholars. He had a broader and more varied scholarship than either Holmes or Emerson. He entered into the death grapple with slavery with a stern and knightly courage and ardour that never swerved or turned aside. His words were "battles for freedom," when freedom most needed defenders. He was the peer of England's greatest scholars, and his fame will brighten with the years.

New soils do not always fatten genius. In a new land the activities of the people are expended in subduing the wilderness, in building great cities, and in developing material resources. With this justification it should be no blemish on our patriotism that we esteem Tennyson as greater than Longfellow, and Scott than Cooper. It should not shame us that we find a richer, deeper tone in Caledonia and Bannockburn, and that they crowd so closely in our affections the songs of our own lands. We have much didactic verse and dainty verse and here and there an anthem full of power, but few of our poets have put such inspirations into verse as Scott, and Tennyson, Burns, and Kipling. It may be that Columbia lingers too long in the market place listening to the music of the ticker and the song of the stockjobber, forgetting the dreams and inspirations that can alone make her children great.

Is it not a question whether our battle hymn has yet been written? *Yankee Doodle* is a silly jingle; *The*

Star Spangled Banner is of limited compass, *Marching Through Georgia*, and some other war songs are a mere matter of music without fit words, and besides they cannot be as well sung in Georgia as in Wisconsin. Few of our patriotic songs will be long remembered although they are dressed in stirring music for the mob. They have but a spark of that immortal fire that blazes in Kipling's latest verse, or in Tennyson's epic, the battle of the one against the fifty-three. Our Spanish War has no poet, although it has inflicted upon us any amount of doggerel and raphsodical music. There was no residium of verse after our war of 1812, and the Mexican war was not provocative of poetry. Perhaps the American Muse was ashamed of that conquest and remained silent even over the glories of Chapultepec and Monterey. I had almost forgotten a song however, with some fine lines in it written by one Hoffman:

> We were not many, we who pressed
> Beside the brave who fell that day;
> But who of us has not confessed
> He'd rather share their warrior rest
> Than not have been at Monterey.

This seems to be the solitary poet of the Mexican War. Who hath remembrance of him now? In our first struggle for freedom, no Kœrnor turned the soldier's barracks into temples where liberty was deified in song. The battle against slavery called out some stormy verse, yet how little we now remember of the scathing passion, the tender, burning words, that Whittier and Longfellow breathed over the wrongs of our bondmen. Some of our jewels it is true are covered with later rubbish. Like a dimly remembered song heard in remote childhood is that eloquent fragment of Emerson's, commencing:

By the rude bridge that arched the flood.

Joaquin Miller's *Song of Peace* is not half so well known as the *Recessional*. We seem to miss the nearer music and remember best the rival lines of Scott and Burns and Kipling.

Upon what meat do these islanders feed that they have such power to charm us with their songs, and make us forget old wrongs, old feuds and old battles? It may be their ocean empire with its outposts on every main. The declamations of our schoolboys bind the race together and annul the bitterness sown by politicians. When we turn from the American poet to his English likeness we are apt to find an enlarged edition.

Whittier's poetry is a crystal winding brook, reflecting summer days and moonlit nights, and the leaf and flower of forest and meadow. But

Tennyson's verse is a river running in stormier measure, and mirroring a larger life. Nature has dealt kindly with us; she has given us sunnier days and mightier lakes and rivers, but in partial mood she has added an Attic savour to the wind that blows across the island kingdom that our more arid breezes have not. The Mississippi Valley lacks several things to make it a place of poetic inspiration. Its mountain fringes lie a thousand miles apart with a flat between. It has no ruins, no traditions, no history except the new and yeasty product begun since our possession of it. Very early, no doubt the human family sent out some meager outposts to this continent. A thousand generations have since flitted through its forests, yet they have died like the cave bear and made no sign. Their literary remains consist in a few attenuated traditions. Even Cooper's book, or artificial, Indian could furnish no theme for the poet. Longfellow tried to fuse this stubborn personality of the Red Brother into song, with something of a success considering the material, but the form of his verse is a long, oft-repeated chant, with the monotonous rythm of the prayer-drums at a Chippewa corn dance. At such a festival, the prayer-drums booming through the wilderness, typify the Indian character. It is an unchanging, ceaseless roll that carries with it the somber unchanging history of the race. It has no vital, living music in it. It belongs to and is a part of the unchanging forests and prairies, and the endless flow of lonely streams where nature broods alone over her own and all things remain as in the first day. Centuries of silence and shadow have passed over this race, and yet its history can be read in a few scattered arrow heads. Such a people could not fatten a soil with legend and story.

I fancy Scott and Burns would have sung no songs had they been born on Bark River Flats, their only indigenous inspirations and occasional flint spear point, or an ancient Indian trail blazed through the forest. They owed all to the mountains of Scotland, her heathery hills and moors, her tarns and brooks peopled with the legends of men outworn. For them a thousand rude singers from the cave-man down had been building a rich alluvium of romance and story. In such a soil poets grow spontaneously and involuntarily. Poetry is an exotic in a flat country and not of natural growth. Mountains have always been a great boon to letters; the gods dwelt on a mountain, and the muses on a high hill. The level plains and flat surfaces of earth have always been the abode of cattle herders and uninspired men. Burns was not a sudden creation; his poetry was in the nature of inherited wealth. He was the heir of many singers, and all the currents of Scottish poetry from the earliest times converged in him. Whittier says:

> I saw the same blithe day return,
> The same sweet fall of even,
> That rose on Wooded Cragie-burn,
> And sank on Crystal Devon.
>
> I matched with Scotland's heathery hills
> The sweetbriar and the clover,
> With Ayr and Doon my native rills
> Their wood-hymns chanting over.
>
> Give lettered pomp to teeth of Time.
> So Bonny Doon but tarry,
> Blot out the epic's stately rhyme,
> But spare his Highland Mary.

Whittier wrote some of the sweetest minor poetry in our language, but he could not transplant to the banks of the Susquehannah, or the Connecticut, the ruined castle of Scotland with its thousand-year-old volume of human life, or the myriad legends that throng the banks of the Doon and the Ayr. His song to Burns is a tribute to the richer life, to the deeper power and passion of Scotland's poet. It is the generous tribute of a poet who stands in a new land barren of tradition, to the land hoary with age and recorded legend.

In our first half-century we had great soldiers and orators and statesmen, but the crop of letters was scanty. There must have been many unsung Odysseys in the lives of those hardy adventurers who came with Raleigh and Smith, and whose descendants later drifted down the Ohio and the Mississippi and over the plains, driving the Indian and the buffalo before them. But we had no Homers to put this pioneer wonder-land into verse. Life was too stern and exacting and pitched in too intense a key, so we built literature slowly in our pioneer age. This early poverty had its effect on the really great builders like Longfellow and Cooper, who came later.

www.ingramcontent.com/pod-product-compliance
Lightning Source LLC
Chambersburg PA
CBHW020800230426
43666CB00007B/776